Hickory: Then & Now
A Complete History

Other books from Redhawk Publications

Hickory

THEN & NOW

1870 — 2020

A Complete History

Richard Eller

REDHAWK
PUBLICATIONS

Redhawk Publications
2550 US Hwy 70 SE
Hickory, NC 28602

Robert Canipe, Editor-in-Chief rcanipe@cvcc.edu

Ordering Information:
Quantity sales. Special discounts are available on quantity purchases by corporations, associations, and others. For details, contact the publisher at the address above.

Printed in the United States of America

ISBN: 978-1-952485-17-6

First Printing

For Claudia

The challenges of keeping a city on the move has caused Hickory to rethink its identity. Setbacks in employment and the dubious distinction of opioid use had caused city leaders to take a moment to plan for a change of trajectory, bringing about several new initiatives to enliven and revitalize.

As the city of Hickory looks to its future, a number of innovations are in the works to prepare for it. The mindset of more roads for automobile traffic, a hallmark of the era when Hickory celebrated its centennial, has given way to a more healthy and less strenuously paced alternative. They call it the Hickory Trail.

By the mid-2010s, Hickory began to examine the trend of major American cities offering walking space between its many attractions. In 2016, city council commissioned a bond referendum to seek funds to provide a sprawling network of "multi-use trails" connecting landmarks all across the city. After the bonds passage, a period of input and planning was followed by the official groundbreaking of the "City Walk" in 2019, to connect Lenoir-Rhyne University with Union Square. The project includes a pedestrian bridge over busy Highway 127 and will parallel the railroad line that rolled into Hickory Tavern ten years before the town was incorporated and established a main transportation source.

City Walk was just a first step. Plans for an extensive network of paths were developed to connect a range of amenities including the "Book Walk," a point of travel between Ridgeview Library and Patrick Beaver Memorial Library at the Salt Block. Also "Old Lenoir Walk" proposed to connect the downtown area with one of Hickory's most important but untapped resources within its city limits, the Catawba River.

Since the construction of Oxford Dam in the 1920s, a lake was formed that provided not only a water source for the city but also recreational opportunities in its waters. Lake Hickory saw the creation of Geitner Park near its banks as well as some residential growth but the city has taken a new interest in the area, looking to make "their water a competitive asset." "The Riverwalk" has been created to develop that asset, creating a thoroughfare that will venture out over the water with a bridge along the trail. Connecting to the Old Lenoir Walk, it will offer another important feature of Hickory for its citizens to enjoy.

Housing in Hickory is even taking a new twist. For generations, citizens have looked to the neighborhoods for housing with the downtown commercial district distinctly separate. In late 2019, all that changed. With the approval of city council, a new $19 million mixed use complex has gone up, just across the street from city hall. One North Center will provide housing and apartments for those seeking to live downtown. Intended for "young professionals and other residents looking for rental options, modern amenities and walkable access to Hickory's revitalized downtown," the retail-residential mix offers a new urban living experience. As City Manager Warren Wood explained, One North Center "will be a first-of-its-kind downtown development that will accommodate the burgeoning demand for rental property with close proximity to the City Walk and Book Walk, as well as restaurants, the farmer's market, merchants, craft beer establishments and live music venues."

Other focal points in the area surrounding downtown Hickory are L.P. Frans Stadium and the Hickory Regional Airport. Both are popular attractions with the Hickory Crawdads and the Aviation Museum offering unique amenities. With the construction of another pedestrian bridge across the busy and soon to be revamped Highway 321 bridge area, an "Aviation Walk" has been added to the system to allow walkers and bicyclists a way to access those destinations creating even further options for those who live in and visit Hickory, as well as a healthy means of getting there.

The biggest future attraction to the river area will be the expansion of Geitner Rotary Park in what has been described as "the largest single donation in the city's history." Robert Lackey and his family sought an appropriate way to honor his late wife Diedra, by creating an expansive complex of attractions for the people of Hickory to enjoy and utilize. The Diedra Lackey Memorial Park project plans to include "a public event space that will house a conservatory, amphitheater, meeting and office space, at one end of the Riverwalk." The public/private partnership seeks to draw families and users of the trail to Lake Hickory.

As a driver of economic activity, Hickory has always been at the forefront of business development, either as a wagon maker, textile or furniture manufacturing outlet, or wholesale food distributor. On a plot of land with planned activity that dates back before the licensing of the "ordinary" of Hickory Tavern. Actually, it was Catawba County's first proposed city.

Ulrich Krauter (or Crowder as his last name was anglicized) was a German immigrant who came to the region around 1763. The following year he received a grant from the King of England as part of the Granville District, giving Krauter 450 acres. Twenty-five years later he tried to sell off parcels, advertising far and wide to attract settlers to then, Lincoln County. Krauter's planned city of "Ulrichsburg" was never realized. He died soon after he plotted out his development, but the area retained the name, also being called Crowdertown.

Under the designation of Park 1764, a reference to Krauters original land grant, Hickory began to create its next generation of industry. "Zoned for office and light industrial," the 270-acre site has continued to sign-on partners since its creation to house a variety of activities. Corning Cable, a radiopharmaceutical manufacturer, and an automotive parts maker are all tenants of the new business park, located on Startown Road, just south of Catawba Valley Community College.

None of these initiatives were cheap. Hickory residents passed a $40 million bond in 2016 to fund each endeavor, which has grown to over $100 million with additional grants and gifts. The success of the bond referendum demonstrated the confidence Hickory residents had in their town to grow. Their heritage bespeaks a bullish nature that always bets on the future. As the wagers of their ancestors have paid off to their benefit, the current city pushes its chips back to the table, putting its money on the future.

Once again, Hickory righted its ship to look forward, to create an inviting future. As it did from the days of the tavern, the invitation brought new Hickoryites ready to weave their thread into the fabric of the city. In 2017, Kipplinger's Personal Finance listed Hickory as one of the top ten destinations in the nation for retirees. With the summer farmer's market, the annual Oktoberfest, Lowes City Park, all in and around Union Square, folks like Charles and Gwen Elmore decided to spend their golden years, enjoying all Hickory had to offer. As observers, who chose to relocate, they may have had the best take on what it was like to live in Hickory. They said, "People here, as a rule, are so kind and not in such a hurry." In a world divided by urban frenzy and rural isolation, the Elmore's characterization make Hickory a place of balance, personifying the well-used phrase, "Life, well crafted."

https://www.hickorync.gov/content/city-walk-information
https://www.hickorync.gov/content/book-walk;
https://www.hickorync.gov/content/old-lenoir-walk-information
https://www.hickorync.gov/content/riverwalk-information
https://www.hickorync.gov/content/plans-announced-downtown-hickory mixed-use-community-development
https://www.hickorync.gov/content/aviation-walk-information
https://www.hickorync.gov/content/lackey-project;
https://www.hickorync.gov/sites/default/files/documents/Presentations/Lackey%20Project%2010-15-19%20FINAL.pdf

https://www.hickorync.gov/sites/default/files/Government/
Departments/Communications/CraftingHickory2017.PDF;
https://www.catawbacountync.gov/site/assets/files/2490/
startown_finalplan.pdf https://www.hickorync.gov/content/
park-1764-information
https://www.hickorync.gov/sites/default/files/Government/
Departments/Communications/CraftingHickory2017.PDF

What explains Hickory's vigor? Its drive? Its ability to bounce back after times of trial and recreate itself stronger than before. There are, no doubt, many factors that, when each generation was called upon to answer came up with solutions borne of their time and their energy. But most have a common thread. Pride mixed with tenacity were always key factors in the answer Hickory gave to trouble. The mental attitude of the people steadied them in any storm, be it flood, epidemic or economic downturn. They also were confident enough in their own skin to welcome newcomers and adapt to a new idea that offered the city an even better future. It's a part of the character of the city since the days of the tavern. Through the Victorian Age and right up to today, the push of Hickory was to work today to create a better tomorrow.

In a city where many of the important landmarks are now gone, it may seem difficult to construct a history. Many significant events have been swept away with the rubble of old houses, churches and businesses. But that drive says something important about the character of Hickory. People looked forward, not content to rest on their laurels, always excited to witness the next event that would build a greater city. In that environment it has been an adventure to crack open the long forgotten books, newspapers, stories on what happened and draw conclusions about what it took to make Hickory what it is.

We, as humans do the same. On birthdays (usually ending with a zero) we look over our shoulder at all that we have experienced, the formative events that made us who we are today. At this sesquicentennial of Hickory, the time has come to do just that, reminding ourselves of how it all came to be. At one point, the city predicted for itself a 21 story building in the downtown area by 1948. It still has yet to be constructed, but what it lost in modest skyscrapers it gained as the stage for several events of national stature, including a response to polio and the center of whole industries including fiber optic cable and furniture.

On the whole, the twentieth century was very good to Hickory. Many people who came liked what they saw. From a tavern in a lonely wilderness came a city boasting a population of 25,000 by the time of its centennial in 1970. After another half century the number zooms past 40,000. For most, Hickory is big enough to be interesting and small enough to be friendly, an admirable combination.

§

Putting your finger on what makes "Hickory Hum" (once upon a time their slogan with a plural on 'hum') remains elusive. This history does not attempt to explain the meaning of life. Really, no work can. It does however attempt to take the town's pulse over time and report its findings, to you, the family that makes up Hickory now. Why does Hickory have a confusing street grid? What made Hickory a mecca in western North Carolina? How did the city become home to furniture? Hosiery? Textiles? Cable? All were the worthy pursuits of the men and women who came before us, giants and scoundrels, gamblers and hard workers who bet on Hickory in a big way. Today we can cash in on their certainty that Hickory was a place worth investing in. It is up to us to take those winnings and invest again for surely the citizens of Hickory on its bi-centennial will judge us as we judge those who came before.

Here's how L.C. Gifford, longtime editor of the Hickory Daily Record put it when he looked back:

> "There are no strangers in Hickory. From the earliest time the welcome sign has always been put out to those who are willing, ready and anxious to contribute their best for the good of all. Actually, we believe, the spirit of Hickory has been evident since its beginning, is about the same as that expressed in the engraving at the Statue of Liberty: '...Give me your tired, your poor...'
>
> In brief, as we see it, the attitude here is not who or what your parents are or were; not what church you belong to, but rather 'Do your thing, do it well and help us make Hickory a better place for all.'
>
> Our people, inheriting deep religious convictions, dream boldly. For this reason—or because of it— we believe that these dreams will be translated into reality and bring growth along the lines of better living for all. We think this growth will continue even at a greater rate during the next century - our tomorrows."

When the 21-story skyscraper comes, we can take pride in the fact that we, along with those recounted in these pages, helped build it.

Richard Eller, June 2020

If you would forget your woes
　　"Come to Hickory"
If you seek a town that grows
　　"Come to Hickory"
Hickory's climate is the best
North or South or East or West —
If you want to work or rest,
　　"Come to Hickory!"

If a social life you crave
　　"Come to Hickory"
If your dollars you would save
　　"Come to Hickory"
Handsome churches you will see
Finest schools we all agree,
If contented you would be
　　"Come to Hickory!"

Here you'll find the queen of flowers
　　"Come to Hickory"
Roses wet with April showers,
　　"Come to Hickory"
All the summer-long they blow,
Here the fragrant violets grow,
Fine chrysanthemums we show —
　　"Come to Hickory!"

Public spirit you will find —
 "Come to Hickory"
Everyone you meet is king
 "Come to Hickory"
Charming girls so sweet and gay,
Manly boys, our hope and stay
Never wish to go away —
 "Come to Hickory!"

Clubs for women, clubs for men —
 "Come to Hickory"
Clubs that number five times ten,
 "Come to Hickory"
Men and women, kind and true,
Do just what they say they'll do,
Waiting here to welcome you,
 "Come to Hickory!"

from "Songs in Many Keys" Emma Ingold Bost

Hickory (Tavern). A town, a city, a regional hub, the center of a metro area began as a lonely wayside inn, a place of respite that gave weary travelers a meal and a bed, and readied them for a further trek into the wilderness. In the mid-eighteenth century, the land leading to the Appalachian Mountains was known as the backcountry, scarcely explored, it was free for the taking. The migration to settle Colonial America had begun and Hickory Tavern served as its rest stop.

In the early eighteenth century, few pioneers had migrated far enough to cross the Catawba River and settle the area, though they were heading in that direction. Adam Sherrill and his family forded the watery barrier around 1747 to be the first. By then, Henry Weidner had likely hunted in the region, but he had yet to stay. The territory was bountiful, only seen by the eyes of the Indians, mostly Catawba. With the river as their base, they disputed boundaries with the Cherokee for decades prior to the arrival of the Europeans. After that came the Spanish, under Juan Pardo. His band was likely the first non-native group to pass through, but they were searching, not settling. The Scots and Germans had different aims. They wanted to claim the land for their own, put down roots and bend the landscape to their needs.

The ridge line upon which Hickory would be built was claimed by first by William McMullin, whose land grant totaled 650 acres. Through the 18th century the land passed through several hands, ending up with Henry Weidner's descendant Henry Robinson, who owned the vast expanse that would later occupy downtown Hickory.1

Within a few decades of Sherrill's crossing of the Catawba, traffic increased. A road was needed. Already, wagons heading out from places as varied as Philadelphia and Charleston carried a variety of homesteaders toward finding a piece of the untamed wilderness to claim as their own. They could harness it for food and livelihood. Civilization, however, only took them so far, like to the frontier town of Salisbury. Further in, lay danger but also good land. In 1769, a path to the west was mapped out and construction began, to carry migrants looking for a new home, a stake for them and their families.

The journey was long and arduous and needed a stopover. Sometime, around 1784, John Bradburn, petitioned his local government (the county of Lincoln had been created in 1777 with Lincolnton as its county seat) to allow him to build an "ordinary," an Enlightenment -era term for a 'public house' or hotel, to provide rest and refreshment for sojourners heading to places like Old Fort, the westernmost outpost at the very foot of the ascending Appalachians. No one knows what Bradburn initially called his hostelry, but it became known regionally as Hickory Tavern.

The trail, known as the Silver Creek Road, established a path very much followed by latter day First Avenue in Hickory. Before its construction, one early Hickory resident, Major J.L. Latta called the hilltop on which Hickory Tavern was built "Bolick's Dry Ridge." J.L. Click, one of Hickory's first newspapermen described the ridge as "sparsely settled and was a wilderness covered with grass in which bears, deer, and all kinds of game roamed."2 That ridge top, upon which the city later emerged, with its center of Union Square, would one day prompt boosters to claim living on that hill offered superior health, and thus a better life than any territory surrounding it.3

A stop at Hickory Tavern offered relief from the wagon or stagecoach ride into the uncertain terrain of western North Carolina. The "ordinary" offered its clientele a meal, a beverage, and a bed to help them recharge and ready themselves for the next leg of their journey. As drivers approached, they bugled their coming, alerting tavern workers to ready services for a new batch of customers. While travelers ate, drank, and slept, the staff changed and fed the horses at the tavern's nearby stable, thought to be located approximately where a later conveyance business stood called Harper Motor Company. In the early 21st century, it became the home of Jackson Group Interactive.4

Hickory Tavern gained its name from its proximity to a hickory tree, that much observers can agree upon. Whether it was a single tree located near the tavern's entrance or a grove of hickory trees, also located nearby, remained an argument between even the town's earliest residents. And they saw the actual building before its demise.

Other stories survive as well, less substantiated and less flattering, but still plausible about how Hickory got its name. One says that since a number of Germans settled the area, they reused a name from Lancaster, Pennsylvania. Just outside of Philadelphia, Lancaster was once called Hickory. Originally named for the Hickory Indians, a small band connected to the Delaware, Lancaster's name change freed up its usage for application elsewhere, possibly in the western foothills of North Carolina.5

The most outlandish reason for Hickory's tavern getting its moniker floated down over years comes from the relationship of one-time tavern owners. One printed story claims that "way back yonder in the past" there was "an aged couple" who ran the inn:

They did not at all times 'pursue the even tenor of their way,' in sweet domestic tranquility. They were brave and settled their family discussions, which were many, by mutual tussle and hair-pulling. The racket at this old house many times attracted the attention of the traveler, who on approaching would find the two in fierce combat, both using hickory withes (switches) as implements of war. Such uncivilized conduct naturally gave the place fame, and travelers consequently dubbed the place 'Hickory Tavern'.6

The establishment of Hickory Tavern, even with a pair of cantankerous innkeepers, came as its visitors were getting used to being citizens of the United States of America, not subjects of the British Empire. The tavern served these new Americans as they came in off the trail to fill their stomachs, enjoy a dram, and lay head to pillow for a night. The land to which they headed was now truly theirs to claim. The tavern became a popular spot, especially for the meals served. Visitors regularly commented on the popularity of the menu at Hickory Tavern. One diner, The Reverend Johannes Oertel, on his way to pastor a church in Lenoir, stopped to eat. His son recorded the meal taken by his family. They enjoyed "a dinner of ham, eggs, and cornbread at the 'Tavern,' readying them to cross the Catawba and head north."7

Over the years, ownership of Hickory Tavern changed hands. Documented operators included John Cline and Simon Haas.8 During Oertel's meal, the operator was referred to as "Snediker." The last, and most famous proprietor was Uncle Joe Miller. He took the quizzical, but bold step of placing a sign above the door, intending to welcome all who came. It read "in crude lettering," "Enter(d)ainment for Man and Beast." Miller ran the tavern at the end of its usefulness, when a village had grown up around the outpost. No longer was Hickory Tavern just an oasis to a weary migrant. Instead, houses and a few shops had begun to spring up, creating an embryonic community, destined to become much more.9

The "double log cabin" as Oertel described the building, stood for enough years to attract a substantial, permanent settlement around it. For several decades past its usefulness, the founding location remained, still in the center of the community but no longer central to its vibrancy. Soon enough, the village surpassed its namesake. Dr. George E. Bisanar, Hickory merchant, optometrist, and former mayor, remembered that the original Hickory Tavern consisted of "a big room divided in the middle by a wall. Because the tavern was small, the women all slept in the east side of the loft and the men on the west side." Bisanar and his family came to Hickory after the heyday of the tavern, when the landmark had outlived its usefulness and became vacant. However, he heard the stories of an earlier generation who relished a time when all that was Hickory, pivoted from that one location.10

The original Hickory Tavern, with its look, its placement

and its place in the city's history has been a popular topic of conjecture since the days in which it did business. Photographs taken by Archer McIntosh around 1870 showed the landmark in its final stage. One image was so hazy that it required latter day outlining to define the tavern. That image, shot from the back right corner, depicted a simple log structure, much less ornate and much smaller than later generations imagined. Another photo, from the back left corner revealed a gaping hole in the upstairs loft. Several of Hickory's young men filled the slot with another pointing a pole in their direction. Those images of Hickory Tavern came from the period when the building was being used as a horse barn. Major Latta mourned the passing of Hickory's founding location by saying, "it seems a sacrilege that this ancient inn, whose hospitable walls and sparking wood fires had provided comfort and rest for Z.B. Vance (Civil War governor and US Senator), Josiah Turner (railroad president and politician), T.J. Jarvis (Governor, US Senator, and Ambassador to Brazil) , R.A. Shotwell (conservative newspaperman) and scores of other notables whose name will live as long as North Carolina history, should be desecrated by its conversion into a horse stable, but fate so decreed."11

Unfortunately, no images from the front, as most travelers would have first seen Hickory Tavern, has survived. In 1965, a group of individuals who offered recollections of the building, including George Bisanar, described the structure with a front porch and second story dormers. Others claim no dormers ever graced the front. In its time, the structure also featured a "stick and stone" chimney, meaning wood exterior with a rock lined interior, for cooking. One of the McIntosh photos showed replacement boards where the chimney once stood.12

The importance of the tavern is foundational to the town that later sprang from it. After all, the city looks back on that singular, solitary enterprise as the genesis for all that came after. Without Hickory Tavern, there would be no Hickory. Certainly, the land favored creation of a settlement, but the need for rest, and the hospitality that came with it, served as a base upon which the town could find its reason for existence. Bolick's Dry Ridge was barren no longer. People had come, not for a night, but to stay.

With its location and growing popularity, Hickory Tavern, as a community, grew up mostly independent of the county in which it found itself. Before John Bradburn built his inn, the land went from being a part of Anson County, to Rowan, then the new North Carolina county of Lincoln in 1777. Quickly however, dissatisfaction began to brew over the length of travel for those in the northern end of the Lincoln County to its seat of local government in of Lincolnton. A secession movement led by upper end residents resulted in the creation of a new county in late 1842, Catawba. Newton emerged as a planned city in the center, the ideal location for the county seat. The tavern and its meager surroundings was too small to even be considered, plus its location, tucked up in the northeast corner of Catawba County would not have appeased those looking for a central location.

Ironically, Hickory Tavern eventually grew to become its own focal point. With its location, the people who came there found themselves in an emerging mecca that welcomed trade and anyone with a plan to better themselves. By the middle of the 19th century, Hickory Tavern was a wayside no more. The promise of its future began to remove the village from the shadow of its county seat to the east. Recognized for the opportunity it offered, Hickory Tavern reached across county borders to bring traders together, creating a larger network for itself than just Catawba County. In fact, the tavern was so far to the west in Catawba County that one observer placed it in Burke.13

The event that established Hickory Tavern as a place of fast growth with a promise of future success came with two iron rails and a bundle of cross ties. In the coming mechanized age, efforts to reach farther into the western portion of North Carolina brought the building of a railroad in the late 1850s. The first publicly printed mention of a place called Hickory Tavern came as a stop along that line.14 Thanks to the establishment of the tavern with its geographic prominence, planners used the ridge line to construct the Western North Carolina Railroad, intersecting it with the Silver Creek Road as again, a stopover. If the tavern and its environs had served patrons of the stage line, why couldn't it also serve as a welcoming respite for rail riders. The original design called for the continued laying of track to the west, but with the coming of the Civil War, construction suspended, leaving Hickory Tavern as the last point of civilization. The circumstance of southern secession caused the line to stop before reaching Morganton, a fortunate event for citizens of the tavern. For the duration of the war, Hickory Tavern Depot, sometimes called Hickory Station, became the end of the line, helping the budding village take on a significance larger than its actual size.

First homes, then businesses began to accumulate as travelers chose to become residents. Henry Link built the first house, on the western end of what became Union Square. He also became the first postmaster in Hickory, storing unclaimed mail at his home. Each day in front of the Link house, a crowd gathered as Henry would call the name of each recipient. Some raised their hands for their own letters, some for others they knew who were not there, with a promise to deliver. The informal practice demonstrates how small the community was in those days. When the train arrived, people stopped to see who got off. As more did, the haphazard arrangement for mail pickup changed. By the spring of 1860, Hickory Tavern was large enough to warrant an official post office from the United States government. Railroad agent for the new line, Adolphus L. Shuford, was offered the job of first Hickory postmaster. But he was busy with the comings and goings of both passengers and freight and declined the offer. The job went to Andrew Lindsay.15

The wide spot along the Silver Creek Road that spawned the tavern and brought the railroad attracted a range of people. Recognizing opportunity, William Hale established a mercantile business on the other side of the tavern and down the road a ways, well before the rail line came through, making himself Hickory's first merchant.16 Some were newcomers to the region, others were more local. For example, the Shuford family had come with the wave of those first pioneers, living for generations south of the current city. When activity began to increase in Hickory Tavern, brothers A.L. Shuford and A.A. Shuford noticed.

Both moved into town to establish themselves and cast their lots with the new location.

The arrival of the Shuford brothers to Hickory Tavern came as the world around them was in flux. That spring folks in the village were faced with two secession movements. In addition to North Carolina marching out of the Union, locals moved to create the new county of Ellis. They offered Hickory Tavern the opportunity to pull together its regional tentacles as a centerpiece to become the new county seat. Ellis County intended to carve off portions of Caldwell, Burke, Catawba and Alexander counties. The State Journal in Raleigh encouraged the effort and a bill in the General Assembly sought to make it official. The new county would be named for Governor John Ellis, who told President Abraham Lincoln after the fall of Fort Sumter that he would get no troops from North Carolina to stop the rebellious southern states from leaving the Union. He, in fact, would join them in their departure.

The secession of Hickory Tavern from Catawba County, like that of North Carolina from the United States, did not succeed. But the Ellis County effort elevated the reputation of Hickory. With an eye toward the town becoming a new county seat, the Raleigh paper wrote that "since the Western N.C.R.R. has been built through their midst, a brisk and thriving little town has sprung up at Hickory Tavern Depot, the contemplated county seat, it being geographically about the centre of the proposed Ellis county." The community offered great promise. Saying Hickory Tavern "is destined to be one of the best trading points in the western part of the State," the writer noted that geographically, "it is the only point of easy access to all the Northwestern counties."17

Hickory Tavern offered a variety of advantages that made it attractive. First, a few miles to the northwest of the spot from which the town sprung, was located one of the best fording sites of the Catawba River. Known as the "horse ford" (meaning it was crossable on horseback), opened an entrance to the sparsely settled portion of the foothills. Beyond the river was "twenty miles of miserable road" as Rev. Oertel called it, that took hardy travelers to Lenoir and the mountain towns of northwestern North Carolina. Trade created traffic headed in both directions, up and down what is now Highway 321, north of Hickory. For the minister, coming from Tarrytown, New York, Hickory served as the jumping off point to his destination. Farmers headed south with wagons loaded with produce to sell. The central marketplace to sell all the goods they could raise, be it animal, vegetable or mineral was Hickory.

To the northeast of town, eight miles away in upper Catawba County, another amenity offered folks a reason to visit. Sulfur springs offered waters that were of "the most rare and excellent qualities and not surpassed by any." Visitors began to seek out the springs with the plan to spend their summers in and around the rejuvenating springs. One newspaper said "we believe this place is destined to become a great centre of resort for our Eastern and Southern friends," making the railroad stop at Hickory Tavern Depot the only route to get there. As the town searched for its own identity, it became known in the early days as the closest railroad stop to the healing springs nearby.

For a multitude of reasons, the town offered hope of

things to come. Perched on the hill as it was, Hickory Tavern had much to provide for those who came. Like the ordinary that spawned it, the community sought the potential to invigorate all who came, offering them opportunities limited by their own imaginations. But the opportunities that lay within Hickory Tavern would have to take a back seat to coming conflict. The issue of county secession paled in comparison to North Carolina leaving the United States and becoming a member of the Confederate States of America. The American Civil War brought a tangle that would both help and hurt the aspirations of Hickory Tavern.

1   https://npgallery.nps.gov/GetAsset/9e692705-21d4-486f-8930-
00e474c387da; "History of Hickory", HDR, October 30, 1936, reprinted in "Lost Hickory: A Compendium of Vanished Landmarks" by Leslie Keller, Hickory Landmarks Society, p. 147-148.

2   "History of Hickory", HDR, October 30, 1936, reprinted in "Lost Hickory: A Compendium of Vanished Landmarks" by Leslie Keller, Hickory Landmarks Society, p. 147.

3   "Hickory's Beauty Preserved", HDR, September 11, 1965, p. 5-B.

4   J.L. Latta, "History of Hickory", HDR, October 30, 1936, reprinted in "Lost Hickory", p. 147.

5   Charles J. Preslar, Jr., "A History of Catawba County," 1954, Rowan Printing Company, Salisbury, NC, p. 343-4.

6   "Tough But Not Rough", Weekly State Chronicle (Raleigh), October 27, 1883, p. 1.

7   W.W. Scott, "Annals of Caldwell County", News Topic Print, 1930, p. 42.

8   Charles J. Preslar, Jr., "A History of Catawba County," 1954, Rowan Printing Company, Salisbury, NC, p. 343.

9   W.W. Scott, "Annals of Caldwell County", News Topic Print, 1930, p. 42; "History of Hickory", HDR, October 30, 1936, reprinted in "Lost Hickory:

A Compendium of Vanished Landmarks" by Leslie Keller, Hickory Landmarks Society, p. 151; Pamela Whitener, "Structure Believed Erected in Last Decades of 1700s", Hickory Daily Record (HDR), June 6, 1970, p. 1, 9.

10   "Hickory's Beauty Preserved", HDR, September 11, 1965, p. 5-B; Pamela Whitener, "Structure Believed Erected in Last Decades of 1700s", Hickory Daily Record (HDR), June 6, 1970, p. 1, 9; "Seniority Enjoyed by Quintet of Union Square Merchants", "Hickory's Beauty Preserved", HDR, September 11, 1965, p. 5-B.

11   Leslie Keller, "Lost Hickory", p. 110.

12   "Which is the Original Hickory Tavern", HDR, September 11, 1965, p. 5-B.

13   Fayetteville Weekly Observer, October 8, 1860, p. 1.

14   "Time Table: Western N. Carolina Rail Road", Iredell Express, October 5, 1860, p. 3. Icard and Morganton were both further stops along the line but Hickory Tavern remained much more of a substantially organized community than Icard and the rail line did not fully extend to Morganton which required transfer of goods, assisting the choice of Hickory as a preferred destination tremendously.

15   Pamela Whitener, "Mail Service Available To Hickory, in 1846, Continuous Since 1848", HDR, (Early History Edition), June 6, 1970, p. 14. By 1846, mail began to arrive in the area, addressed to residents of Hickory Tavern. But for a couple of years correspondence didn't reach the tavern. Instead, William Hale took possession at a village called Chestnut Oak, thought to be located in what is now southeast Hickory. Hale's store handled Hickory mail until Link took over.

16   "History of Hickory", HDR, October 30, 1936, reprinted in "Lost Hickory: A Compendium of Vanished Landmarks" by Leslie Keller, Hickory Landmarks Society, p. 147.

17   Semi-Weekly State Journal (Raleigh), February 9, 1861, p. 2.

The Civil War put the growth of Hickory on hold. By the spring of 1861, when the fighting started, houses and a few businesses dotted the lots around the old tavern, which was still in operation. But young men began to disappear from the community. Adolphus "Dolph" Shuford remained to run the depot for the railroad. However, his younger brother, not yet 20 years old, marched from his new hometown to Newton and volunteered to protect his state from the anticipated federal invasion that many thought President Lincoln would unleash.

The first two years of the war passed quietly around the tavern. By 1863, two events conspired to stir activity in the community. Town folk wanted to incorporate. Led by Dolph Shuford, Henry Link (first postmaster), Dr. J.R. Ellis, and merchant Lee Elias, a petition was sent to the North Carolina General Assembly to grant Hickory Tavern a charter with all the "rights, privileges, powers, and immunities, conferred upon commissioners of incorporated towns" by state government. The petition went into record for consideration by the General Assembly on December 12, 1863. Town limits of one thousand yards from the railroad depot were stipulated and it looked as though the momentum of the town prior to the war might continue.1

But what was intended to be the start of Hickory Tavern, or as some were calling it "Hickory Station," stalled. The stated reason was that the appointed commissioners failed to properly qualify. One of them apparently left town during the period, but it is unlikely that such a move upended Hickory's hopes of incorporation. The possible culprit was the war itself. With the state legislature locked in a war, the push for recognition of Hickory Tavern became a matter to be tabled in the face of the declining fortunes of the Confederacy as 1864 approached. Not only did the General Assembly control the contribution of North Carolina's war materiel to the effort, lawmakers also battled with the Confederate government over those contributions. Governor Zeb Vance tried to hold back some of its goods, like uniforms, while CSA president Jefferson Davis sought more. Major Latta summarized it simply, writing that the appointed commissioners "failed to qualify, owing to the exigencies of war."2

The year 1863 also brought a new business alongside the railroad tracks. The Confederate government needed locations all across the South to store the goods it needed to supply armies in their fight for recognition. CSA Major E.M. Todd rode in on the Western North Carolina Railroad to build a commissary on the south side of the tracks. Before construction was complete, Todd and his workers had constructed four buildings, housing all manner of goods. Cotton, salt, whiskey, wheat and more were warehoused and ready for shipment to the front lines as needed. Some of the goods were bought in by rail, but many items came from the people who lived in and around the village. Laws enacted by the Confederate government required citizens to contribute a tenth of their annual output and the commissary was designated as the place of deposit.

Prior to the late winter of 1865 the carnage of war remained far away from Hickory Tavern. Newspapers from other cities floated into town telling of the battles and the loss of life that came with them. Young A.A. Shuford found himself involved in many of those fights. Abel Alexander Shuford grew up much the same as his brother, Dolph. He received a basic education at the "field schools" in the area. Serving in Company F of the 23rd North Carolina Regiment, A.A. saw action at most of the major eastern theatre contests including the Seven Days battles where he was severely wounded. He recovered, fought at Fredericksburg and Gettysburg, where he was again wounded. Captured by federal forces, he spent the rest of his time as a prisoner of war at Point Lookout, Maryland. While A.A. sat out the last two years, his brother Dolph assisted Major Todd in the administration of the commissary back in Hickory Tavern.3

Six days after Lee surrendered to Grant at Appomattox Court House, federal cavalry brought war to the doorstep of the town. General George Stoneman launched a raid into the mountain heart of the Confederacy. From Tennessee, Stoneman's cavalry went on the offensive, disrupting activity wherever his men could. Until then, the foothills of western North Carolina had escaped physical destruction. No longer. Circling the region, Stoneman headed for Salisbury, the site of a Confederate prison. He got there after all the Union soldiers had been freed. Heading back west, he decided to split his forces, seeking hidden supplies, but also opportunities for devastation. Colonel William Palmer took a portion of the raiders from Statesville through Taylorsville and to Hickory Station. Their objective was Major Todd's commissary.

Todd had some last minute warning of the arrival of Stoneman's cavalry advance. He attempted to ship out what he could on trains. What he couldn't get rid of by rail, he chose to burn and "promptly set fire to the commissary building, which was soon reduced to ashes." Among the items intended for destruction to keep out of Union hands were "a great number of heavy sacks of salt," as well as "over one hundred barrels of molasses, vinegar and brandy." Union cavalrymen could still see the plume of smoke over the railroad stop as they approached and spurred their horses toward the depot. Civilians in the area saw it too.4

The Confederate government bet that a storehouse in a remote place like Hickory Tavern would be safe from the federals. But Stoneman's Raid proved the Confederacy wrong. In the final days of the war, George Stoneman needed all the Confederate commissaries he could find, if for no other reason than to rebuild his reputation. In 1863, at the battle of Chancellorsville in northern Virginia, Stoneman's cavalry performed badly, failing to keep tabs on Lee's army and allowing Stonewall Jackson's men to maneuver out of their sight and successfully scatter the entire right flank of the Union army. Chancellorsville is remembered as a signature victory for the Confederates, due in part to Stoneman's showing. If that wasn't bad enough, Stoneman managed to get captured in Georgia in 1864. He needed redemption.

The federal contingent arrived at Hickory Tavern too late to do much of anything. Union Captain Henry Weand watched the smoky ruin. He later wrote, "in a military sense it was wise to destroy stores that might be of use to us, but to burn their cotton was rank foolishness." He pointed out that the cavalry would have no way to transport the bales to the North, some as large as 500 pounds in weight. "Everyone recognizes that the rebellion is on its last legs," he added, "and that in a short time they could realize from a waiting market an amount of money that would go far to make up their losses, but a madness seems to make these people believe that in so despoiling themselves, they are in some way hurting us."5

Weand was not talking about the people of Hickory Tavern. In his observations concerning the fire, he referred to Major Everard Moore Todd, the Confederate officer who commanded the commissary and put the torch to it. Todd was a Virginian, a lawyer by training at Harvard, but he never practiced. Instead, he went into his father's business of curing and selling hams.6 His decision to burn the entire commissary complex may have been a fleeting decision, but local folks did not agree, seeing the issue much more as Captain Weand had.

Hickory columnist E.L. Shuford (son of Dolph) recalled the circumstances that spring morning when Major Todd made his fateful choice. Dousing supplies of meat, potatoes and flour with kerosene, he "struck a match and lit out in his buggy leaving behind those to feed the 'Yanks' as best they must." Shuford recalled the grumbling that went on by those left behind. "This wanton destruction incensed the country around and they appealed to Governor Vance to punish Todd." Instead, the major returned to Virginia and a handful of families around the commissary were left to rebuild.7 The issue was personal for many. The goods in storage included their own. The best they could do was to gather up what "scorched and roasted salt" they could after the cavalry left and try to make use of it.8

The aftermath of the war left Hickory Tavern depleted but not destitute. Even with the commissary and all its goods gone, residents still saw a firm foundation upon which they could build a city. Leaders had already made one official attempt to be recognized. After the effort failed they didn't forget. Instead, they waited out the rest of the war and looked for another opportunity. To them, the time seemed right in the summer of 1868. Legislation came before lawmakers in Raleigh. But for a second time inaction on the part of state government prevented the locality from being recognized. A July petition failed to get the Governor William Holden's attention to appoint town commissioners. Unfortunately, Hickory Tavern's municipal matter came to grief again because of bad timing, with turmoil in the eastern part of North Carolina overshadowing efforts in the west.

William Woods Holden had previously served as governor at the end of the war. He was appointed to the job by Reconstruction president Andrew Johnson. He was a Republican, the era's liberal party, which put him very much out of step with former Confederates. After being voted out in 1865, he ran again just as the Hickory Tavern proposal was going forward. His election in the summer of 1868 came as the state adopted a new constitution, a requirement of reentry into the Union. Holden's relationship with the opposition party had never been good but his second term as governor demonstrated just how bad it could get. His entire tenure as chief executive of the state was marked with strife to the point that he became the first governor of any state in the nation to be impeached and removed from office. The 'would be town' remained unrecognized.

Citizens of the tavern kept trying. A third attempt later that year suffered due to the fact that county commissioners failed to appoint judges for a May election. Undeterred, local leaders made a fourth attempt, finally able to navigate the process to successful completion. In the waning days of 1869, the General Assembly named six commissioners (with any three of them sufficient for the task) to conduct an election, scheduled for the first Monday in 1870, January 3rd. On that day, Hickory Tavern the town, selected its first mayor and commissioners to govern.9

Marcus Yoder won election as Hickory Tavern's first mayor. Born around 1840, he was of prime age when the Civil War came in 1861. Less than a year after its start, he signed up with the 46th North Carolina, serving the regiment as a musician throughout the war. With only "modest schooling" during his upbringing, he returned home to start a mercantile business in the new, still unincorporated town. Once Hickory Tavern gained its charter, Yoder held the job of mayor until 1874. During that time he also served as the town's magistrate. "He held court in his store on the west end of Union Square and used his warehouse for a calaboose," a handy consideration of jobs. Married, but with no children, he willed his estate to Zion and Holy Trinity Lutheran Churches for their future growth.10

As initial incorporation came, so did many changes for Hickory. The faithful organized into official bodies and began campaigns to build their individual houses of worship. The Methodists were first, building their church around 1866, as recorded in the minutes of the South Carolina Conference. In 1869, members of the German Reformed

Church established Corinth Evangelical and Reformed Church two blocks north of the railroad tracks. Baptists formally organized their congregation a year later, followed by the Episcopal Church in 1872, and the Lutherans with Holy Trinity four years later. The First Presbyterian Church of Hickory organized with a meeting held at First Methodist in 1873. All of these groups were around much earlier than their official start dates with each making some claim as the first to gather in Hickory Tavern. For example, early Baptists met in homes from about 1860, the year of the arrival of the railroad. Members of Corinth met during that summer in a brush arbor (a temporary edifice). A number of influential business leaders spurred the establishment of Corinth Church including Henry Link, the first unofficial postmaster, and Abel A. Shuford, who was destined to become one of the most prominent and successful of all Hickory citizens.11

Hickory had two Shufords who were driving the town to greater heights. Brothers Dolph and A. A. were part of a family of eleven children born and raised near the banks of Henry Fork. Adolphus Lafayette was the oldest son, born in 1832. He is credited as being a founder and one of Hickory's first residents. Trained as a carpenter, Dolph, as he was known, assisted in construction of the Western North Carolina Railroad as it came through Hickory Tavern. He took the job of station agent for the line and remained there throughout the Civil War. He also served as assistant head of the Confederate commissary. After the war, it was Dolph who loudly promoted the advantages of Hickory Tavern as a destination.12

A few weeks after the town was established, Dolph Shuford corresponded with a Charlotte newspaper about just how great it was to live and work in Hickory. "It is a thriving town of several hundred inhabitants, and has built up since the close of the war," he wrote. He estimated that the number of stores totaled ten, plus a few workshops sprinkled in that "carried everything needed in any part of the country." The elder Shuford brother became an ardent promoter for the town. He put forth a theory that the location of Hickory bested any other community in the region for the welfare of its people.13

"This is one of the healthiest places to be found anywhere," Dolph crowed. Calling the climate "particularly delightful" he explained it by concluding "we are on the top of a mountain, but not conscious of it." He cited the height of Hickory at 1,194 feet above sea level, significantly more elevated than Salisbury to the east and even higher than Morganton to the west and Lenoir to the north. He asserted that the "extraordinary healthfulness" found there put Hickory Tavern in a place he called the "healthy belt." As close as ten miles to the east he saw "miasmic diseases and other malignant distempers common." About the same distance to the west he pointed to "various mountain diseases" such as diphtheria, double pneumonia, pleurisy, and especially those most of all to be dreaded mountain diseases which prevail all year - typhoid fever and rheumatism." As he diagnosed it, those maladies led to "incurable, organic diseases of the heart."14

Later studies of Hickory's elevation confirm at least some of Dolph Shuford's assertions. Hickory is indeed at a higher altitude than surrounding towns. Several certifications by the United States Geological Survey around Union Square place the altitude of Hickory within thirty feet of Dolph's measurement. On top of that hill, Hickory benefits from the shelter provided by the Appalachian Mountains to the west and north from severe weather, a climate in town referred to by old timers as "salubrious." The elevation it enjoys served to offer a refreshment for visitors who saw Hickory in much the same way that twentieth century vacationers saw Blowing Rock, a civilized respite in the North Carolina mountains. Until roads got better, staying in Hickory was as close as one could get to a mountain getaway. Visitors saw Hickory as having better air. Whether it actually protected them from disease has never been proven.15

Dolph Shuford made his case eloquently and no doubt swayed readers who might consider a trip. In addition to extolling the health virtues of the place, he added that his hometown was "destined to be one of the finest business places in western North Carolina." Other business observers agreed. A reporter from the Wilmington Journal, at the time the state's largest city, declared that the growth of Hickory was without precedent in North Carolina, "if we except Durham," putting the town on par with one of the New South's most successful creations.16

Much of what observers attributed to Hickory's future as a center of commerce looked northwest. "I see by an act of the Legislature that there has been money appropriated for the purpose of building a turnpike road through several counties in the West, and among them Caldwell and

Watauga," Dolph commented. He welcomed Hickory as a center of activity, seeing only more advantages for the old tavern as a new business hub. The additional road would certainly improve transportation already funneling into Hickory from across the Horseford Bridge.

Quantifying his argument that Hickory had grown substantially since the railroad came through, Dolph cited a "large increase in freight at this point. It being 200 percent in the last few years." The increase goes, as he said, "to show what an industrious people can and will do, even under many embarrassments such as are generally experienced after a long and ruinous war." Dolph left no stone unturned in debating the value of Hickory as a nucleus for the region. He pointed to iron ore and mineral water, all within a short carriage ride of the town. As station agent for the railroad, he had compiled numbers for all that rail cars shipped out, the exports of Hickory. "Butter 18,170 pounds, eggs 5,140 dozen, beeswax 4,666 pounds, honey 1,780 pounds, bacon 16,898 pounds, apples (green) 253 bushels, oats 879 bushels, rye 637 bushels, corn 6,888 bushels, flour 198 sacks, dried fruits and berries 215,430 pounds, roots and herbs 768,286 pounds, chestnuts, onions, potatoes, flax seed and other miscellaneous articles 300,000 pounds."17

With so much in the way of goods flowing into Hickory Tavern and the railroad shipping it out to a growing consumer market, Dolph Shuford wanted readers to bet and win on the future of the town. He envisioned Hickory as, not just a railroad stop, but as a focal point of the region. Calling upon officers of the Wilmington, Charlotte, and Rutherfordton Railroad to build a line from Lincolnton to

Hickory, he believed "such a connection will be of more benefit to Charlotte than any other road that we know of, because it will tap the Western N.C. Road at an important point." His assessment proved to be right on target for the growing fortunes of Hickory. However, it would be another railroad line that took the bait.18

Dolph Shuford proclaimed Hickory to be an only slightly tapped Eden, inviting anyone with a better idea and a nose suited for the grindstone to come and test their mettle. After his father-in-law built the first brick store in Hickory, around 1860, Dolph bought it and added a second story. The building, demolished in the early 1920s, stood on the wing of eastern Union Square, today part of the downtown parking area. To prove his confidence, he also put down roots for his expanding family of nine children with a lavish two-story farmhouse surrounded by ample fields on the northeastern outskirts of Hickory in 1883, an estate known as Maple Grove. In his pastures, he placed the first Jersey cows brought to North Carolina. But two years later Dolph Shuford was dead, a victim of heart disease. By then, younger brother A.A. Shuford was ready to receive the baton passed to him as bullish advocate of Hickory.19

Following his service in the Confederate army, A.A. returned to the family farm and took up the plow for the growing season of 1865. But when the harvest came in, A.A. chose to join his brother at Hickory Tavern. He spent some time learning the ins and outs of retail as a clerk for Lee Elias, a Jewish businessman in downtown Hickory. With $500, A.A. partnered in an early business and took his place with brother Dolph as one of Hickory's "pioneers." On the eve of his 40th birthday, he chose to establish his first industrial business seven miles to the north of Hickory, in Caldwell County. There, with several partners he built a large cotton mill that became instantly successful. From that point forward, A.A. Shuford became an important person in Hickory.20

In public life, the younger Shuford had a 'Midas touch.' Everything with which he associated succeeded. After his businesses prospered, he got politically active, serving beside his brother Dolph as an elected commissioner of Hickory in 1875.21 In less than ten years, he would take a seat in the North Carolina General Assembly.22 Appropriating an idea from his brother, A.A. became involved in bringing a second rail line to Hickory. In 1873, he served as a commissioner for the Chester and Lenoir Narrow Gauge Railroad Company, seeking funds to lay track through downtown Hickory in 1873.23

Both Shufords engaged in downtown retail stores in early Hickory, but they had competition. Other mercantile operations dotted the circle of businesses around the railroad depot, known at the time as Park Place, later Union Square. Abernethy, Yoder and Company established operations prior to incorporation. By 1870, the store offered almost everything needed in life. Food, medicine, leather goods, household supplies, musical instruments, even coffins were all sold out of a building George W. Hahn described as a "large and sprawling wooden structure," that was "situated on a corner with only a dirt path for a sidewalk in front and beside it." A ledger of transactions survived the company itself, complete with an understanding of prices in Hickory's first days. Eggs were ten cents a dozen, beef sold for 12 1/2 cents a pound, and customers could get 32 pounds of corn for 50 cents.24

The year 1870 turned out to be a watershed year for Hickory Tavern. After incorporation in January, the town began to take off in a number of different directions. That year, the first newspaper, the Carolina Eagle began to chronicle the activity of Hickory citizens. The town's first physician to take up residence, Dr. J.R. Ellis began the paper. His brother, W.H. Ellis was an early merchant. An important industry came to town that year, one generally associated with cities to the east in North Carolina. Near the town's livery stable, A.W. Marshall opened a tobacco factory, encouraging local farmers to grow the leaf. Before tobacco ended up in the hands of Duke and Reynolds in Durham and Winston-Salem, respectively, a total of seven tobacco factories operated in Hickory. They made everything from plug (chewing tobacco) to cigars.25

It didn't take long for the name 'Hickory Tavern' to become unwieldy. Three years after the state legislature approved the town's incorporation, the General Assembly considered another charter. This one annulled the establishment of Hickory Tavern in favor of a new moniker; Hickory. Dropping 'tavern' from the official municipal designation, detached the new city, at least somewhat from its past. No longer was the town tied to the wayside where it all started. The new ratification allowed Hickory to reach as far as one mile from its new ground zero, the depot warehouse on the rail line. The new charter prescribed a ruling body of six commissioners to assist the mayor.

Elections were set for the first Monday in May, annually.26

The 'wide spot in the road' image for Hickory had become part of its past, a historical beginning but no longer an apt portrayal of what was going on. A visitor from the Raleigh Weekly State Chronicle commented on the transformation. He remembered an earlier time when "parties going to and from the mountains stopped at the 'Tavern,' rested and regaled themselves in the old fashioned, rudely constructed building erected for their accommodation." He recalled Hickory Tavern as a "little, dull, sleepy place" that had "no attraction for visitors and had no inducement to capitalists." It was, as he said, "Sleepy Hollow." But his 1888 return to Hickory brought a different view. "Improvements are visible on every hand," he admitted. "The paint brush is busy and carpenters have no idle time. Residences and stores are in the process of construction. New enterprises are being started. There is life here. There is activity here. There is no stagnation."27

1   "History of Hickory", HDR, October 30, 1936, reprinted in "Lost Hickory: A Compendium of Vanished Landmarks" by Leslie Keller, Hickory Landmarks Society, p. 156.

2   "History of Hickory", HDR, October 30, 1936, reprinted in "Lost Hickory: A Compendium of Vanished Landmarks" by Leslie Keller, Hickory Landmarks Society, p. 149.

3   Charlotte Democrat, November 11, 1881, p. 2; Newton Enterprise, January 16, 1885, p. 3.

4   "History of Hickory", HDR, October 30, 1936, reprinted in "Lost Hickory: A Compendium of Vanished Landmarks" by Leslie Keller, Hickory Landmarks

Society, p. 149.

5   https://digital.ncdcr.gov/digital/collection/p15012coll8/id/11057; https://stonemangazette.blogspot.com/2015/04/coming-to-fork-in-raid.html.

6   https://www.dhr.virginia.gov/VLR_to_transfer/PDFN-oms/127-5978_E.M.Todd_Company_2002_Final_Nomination.pdf; "Men of Mark in Virginia: Ideals of American Life; A Collection of Biographies of the Leading Men in the State, Volume 5", edited by Lyon Gardiner Tyler, LLD, Men of Mark Publishing Company, Washington, DC, 1909, p. 422
For more on Weand, see William Henry Powell's "Officer of the Army and Navy (volunteer) who Served in the Civil War, L.R. Hamersly & Company, 1893, p. 226.

7   E.L. Shuford, "Hickory Tavern", HDR, April 1, 1919, p. 1.

8   "History of Hickory", HDR, October 30, 1936, reprinted in "Lost Hickory: A Compendium of Vanished Landmarks" by Leslie Keller, Hickory Landmarks Society, p. 149.

9   Charles Preslar, "A History of Catawba County, Charles J. Preslar, Jr., editor, Catawba County Historical Association, p. 345.

10   George W. Hahn, "The Catawba Soldier in the Civil War: A Sketch", 1911, p. 272; "Hickory Past Mayors", HDR, June 6, 1970, Centennial Edition (Hickory Today and Tomorrow), p. 1; "Memory of Marcus Yoder", Hickory Democrat, November 18, 1909, p. 2.

11   "Historic Corinth United Church of Christ One of Oldest In Hickory", "Methodists to Note Anniversary", Church Organized in 1873", "First Baptist, Hickory, Expanding", "Membership More Than 1,200 at Holy Trinity", "Presbyterians Organize Here in 1873", HDR, September 11, 1965, Section C, p. 1-2, 4, 12.

12   https://archive.org/stream/historicalsketchooshuf/historicalsketchooshuf_djvu.txt

13   http://www.hickorylandmarks.org/MapleGrove.asp; "Potentials Seen in 1870", HDR, September 11, 1965, p. 2-E.

14   "Potentials Seen in 1870", HDR, September 11, 1965, p. 2-E.

15   "Hickory Built on Ridges", HDR, September 11, 1965, p. 7E.

16   Piedmont Press, November 26, 1873, p. 2.

17   "Potentials Seen in 1870", HDR, September 11, 1965, p. 2-E.

18   "Potentials Seen in 1870", HDR, September 11, 1965, p. 2-E.

19   https://archive.org/stream/historicalsketchooshuf/historicalsketchoos-huf_djvu.txt; http://www.hickorylandmarks.org/MapleGrove.asp; Leslie Keller, "Lost Hickory: A Compendium of Vanished Landmarks", Hickory Landmarks Society, Inc., 2010, p. 127-8.

20   Charlotte Democrat, November 11, 1881, p. 2; Newton Enterprise, January 16, 1885, p. 3; "History of Hickory", J.L. Latta, HDR, October 30, 1936, republished in "Lost Hickory: A Compendium of Vanished Landmarks", Hickory Landmarks Society, Inc., 2010, p. 149.

21   Raleigh Christian Advocate, May 19, 1875, p. 2; Newton Enterprise, January 16, 1885, p. 3.

22   Newton Enterprise, January 16, 1885, p. 3.

23   Yorkville Enquirer, May 22, 1873, p. 2.

24   Pamela Whitener, "Old Record Proves Entertaining", HDR (Early History), June 6, 1970, p. 2.

25   "Dozen Newspapers Failed to Survive in Hickory", HDR, September 11, 1965, p. 6F; "Tobacco Products Firms No Longer Flourish Here", HDR, September 11, 1965, p. 12F.

26   Charles Preslar, "A History of Catawba County," Charles J. Preslar, Jr., editor, Catawba County Historical Association, p. 345.

27   Weekly State Chronicle (Raleigh), April 20, 1888, p. 1.

"*Last Tuesday a car-loaded with Piedmont Wagons from the Piedmont Wagon Company, Hickory, passed down the Western Road for Danville, Va. On each side of the car was a handsomely painted sign bearing the following inscription: 'Piedmont Wagons The New South is ahead of the Old North and the Great West, Sold by R.W. White, Danville, Va.' The Piedmont Wagon Company is an enterprise in which not only Hickory, but Catawba county and the entire State feels a just pride.'"[1]*

The story, under the title of "Catawba Leads," appeared in the pages of the Newton Enterprise in March of 1886. It heralded Hickory's signature business of the era. In much the same way that the tavern marked the birth of Hickory, Piedmont Wagon marked the birth of industrial Hickory, its creation seminal to the growth that would occur around it.

Piedmont Wagon began as "Ramseur and Bonniwell," a wagon making partnership down on the Catawba River. A native of Philadelphia, George Bonniwell came to Hickory in 1878, looking to find an outlet for his mechanical genius. Andrew Ramseur owned a mill on the banks of the Catawba, near the Horse Ford Bridge and the two began constructing wagons. Production went from fifteen to fifty in a year, quickly outgrowing the mill. In 1880, a group of local investors convinced the pair to relocate to a new factory by the railroad tracks on the western end of Hickory. At that point, former and future mayor J.G Hall took over. From there, production took off. Throughout the 1880s the company was unable to keep up with the orders coming in for the wagons, which were renowned for being sturdy and 'green.'2

The relationship between the company and the town to which it came turned out to be symbiotic. Hickory offered a track-side place from which Piedmont Wagon could ship its product. The town also supplied a labor force to build them. In turn, the factory became the biggest employer at the time and put Hickory on the map. The industrial establishment, on the western end of town became a hive of activity, a sprawling complex with shops for crafting wheels and wagon bodies, as well as wood and iron working areas. Products were painted in a signature green and shipped out daily. By 1883, the Hickory Press had to admit that "there is no other industry here that circulates more money in the community that the Piedmont Wagon Company."3

The arrival of the wagon works came at a pivotal time for the town. By the early 1880s everything had grown in Hickory. A national depression in 1873 held the economy back for a while, but recovery helped Hickory to rebound by the time of the nation's centennial year. Ten years after the Panic of 1873 the population had grown to 1,800 with estimates of "thirty mercantile establishments and a home market unequaled in the western part of the state."4

Those businesses were being served by the Western North Carolina Railroad, but a cheaper alternative was coming. Narrow gauge rail lines received attention in all parts of the United States "on account of their cheapness and their practicability in places where it would not be possible to construct roads of ordinary width."5 As early as 1871, "a narrow gauge railroad from Chester, S.C., to Hickory Tavern, N.C., is being talked of" in South Carolina newspapers.6 By early the following year, a company was incorporated to build the line from Chester through Hickory and into Caldwell County, with the terminus in Lenoir. Using convict labor, the line, remnants of the antebellum Kings Mountain Railroad, began construction in 1873. It took ten years for track to be laid to Newton. Then a deal was struck with the Western North Carolina Railroad to use their line, with a third rail installed for the smaller distance between rails of the Chester and Lenoir. Two days after Christmas in 1883, the first narrow gauge train pulled into Hickory using most of the already established track.7

On the western end of Hickory, the Chester and Lenoir Narrow Gauge line departed the earlier, established railroad at the Piedmont Wagon factory, heading north into Caldwell County and crossing the Catawba in early 1884. Hickory had become the kind of railroad hub Dolph Shuford imagined when he implored the people of Wilmington, Charlotte, and Rutherfordton to come fourteen years earlier. Now traffic poured into Hickory from all four directions. Plus, the mountain trade bringing produce down from the mountains had an easier ride. Eventually, the line would extend into upper Caldwell County near the logging camp town of Mortimer, but no longer was Hickory the end of the line like it was in the days of the Civil War. It was a junction.

It became quickly evident that Hickory was a municipality on the move. Statewide, while other towns reported their haunted houses and fist fights, Hickory extolled "the trade of our merchants" who had greatly increased their traffic "especially in mountain produce, while Piedmont Wagons were "being turned out in great abundance."8 Hickory asked for, and got, an ever widening array of businesses, each managed by an entrepreneur destined to make a go of it, believing they had found a town that would help them in their pursuit.

The most prominent example of the kind of businessman Hickory attracted stepped off the train one sunny afternoon in September of 1886, bent on making his mark. His name was Daniel Webster Shuler and he wanted to start Hickory's first bank. His credentials were sound. After all, he and a partner had already created the Bank of Johnson City (Tennessee) earlier that year and Shuler planned to repeat the feat, on his own, down the mountain.

At the time, there was no formal bank in Hickory. If people needed money, they could go to Shuford's Hardware, where owner A.A. Shuford lent trustworthy souls the funds they needed. It was a good way to move commerce forward, but hardly the kind of institution that shows the town as a city of stature. When Shuler arrived, he pitched his intention around town, and within two months, the Bank of Hickory was doing business, with A.A. Shuford as a supporter.

The Bank of Hickory only began the agenda of Daniel Shuler. Immediately, he organized a campaign to build a grand hotel. The accommodations at the Western Hotel he used when he first arrived alerted him to the need. From there, he backed one project after another to amplify Hickory into the premiere city of western North Carolina.

An insurance company, a timber business, a race track, Hickory's first electric company were all part of Shuler's interests. In addition he improved the fairgrounds, bought interest in a mill, built the finest house in town, spearheaded the building of an opera house (which he managed) and got himself on the board of Piedmont Wagon, all in less than four years. Dolph Shuford's son, E.L., dubbed the period, the "Shuler Era" and never has the city seen such energy and excitement in the person of one man in such a short time.

Everything Daniel Shuler did, he did with flair. The Bank of Hickory was adorned with a mural painted by F.A. Grace, who also used the walls of his Queen Anne style home as a canvas for the artist. His race track, known in that era as a "driving park" figured into his larger scheme to elevate the annual fair and attract spectators from beyond the city limits. When it opened, the Hickory Inn was called "one of the finest in the South."9 For a time, everything Shuler touched turned to gold, and this reflected well on Hickory.

Many people were charmed by the young man from Michigan. He and his wife Maud became a celebrated couple around town, their guests and travels reported regularly in the press. Even his oldest daughter Bessie enjoyed more attention than any other thirteen year old had a right to claim in 1890. That year, Shuler planned to make Fourth of July activities in Hickory memorable. He hired an "aeronaut" who planned to jump from a balloon at over 7,000 feet, and parachute back to the earth. In the preflight era, it was quite a spectacle. However, the feat fizzled when at just over 1,000 feet, Professor McEwen jumped, an underwhelming spectacle. It was a harbinger of what was ahead for Hickory's brightest star.

In mid-August the Bank of Hickory failed. Shuler took to his bed, claiming a heart condition brought on by the bad news. Before midnight, the bank owner succumbed to death, leaving a mess for his wife and depositors to figure out. With a healthy insurance payout, his wife offered to pay off her husband's debts for the right to name the chief teller of a new bank for Hickory that was already in the works at the time of Shuler's failure. A.A. Shuford objected and the losses were never made good. If Shuler's demise was not scandalous enough, six weeks after his passing came a revelation, put forth by his brother that Daniel Shuler faked his own death. Did he or didn't he? Hickory would never know for sure, but the mystery was compounded by the fact that during the following winter, Maud returned to town and had her husband's corpse exhumed from Oakwood Cemetery, returning Daniel Shuler's body to Michigan.

Shuler's arrival and his acceptance by the Hickoryites demonstrated everything the town aspired to be, a progressive, accepting, vigorously motivated city. And whereas Hickory had a coterie of founding fathers, most of whom were local and conservatively guided it to steadily greater heights, Shuler represented what a quantum leap the town could take if it only had visionaries to guide it. The circumstances of the demise of the Bank of Hickory have never been completely sorted out. It started with such promise, a moment for Hickory to crow over its march of progress and yet turned into a catastrophe of gigantic proportions.

Yet, even with the Shuler scandal, Hickory remained undeterred. Daniel Shuler had only proved that not every person could deliver. However, many of his projects propelled the community forward. The Hickory Inn continued to welcome guests in a lavish style, just as the Elliott Opera House attracted patrons from towns across the region with a variety of exhibitions. The electric company brought light to more and more houses in Hickory from its dynamo situation near the Catawba River. In fact, Hickory was among the first cities of the state to offer electricity to its citizens. Shuler left Hickory more prominent and more dynamic than he found it, even if he did not enjoy the fruits of his activity.

By the time of Shuler's exit from the Hickory stage, the town found itself more significantly advanced than ever. The failure of the Bank of Hickory paved the way for a new bank in Hickory, built on more than a stranger coming to town. A citizens' bank had been in the planning stages before the Shuler scandal but its need grew ever more pressing after. According to the bank itself, a group of 14 men subscribed the first $50,000 for the First National Bank of Hickory to begin operations on June 10, 1891. At the head of the group was A.A. Shuford who became president of the bank. A local retail store owner, O.M. Royster was named Vice-President and most interestingly, K.C. Menzies was named cashier for the bank. Menzies had worked for the Shuler bank in a junior capacity. It was the only link between the old bank and the new.

First National of Hickory (later of Catawba County) never acknowledged the existence of a bank in Hickory prior to their creation. However, First National did occupy the offices of the Bank of Hickory for a number of years before tearing it down and on the same spot building a magnificent marble structure on the west wing of Union Square. Much like the Dolph Shuford's store, those wing buildings were demolished in favor of greater parking space between the railroad tracks and line of buildings still existent.10 Headquarters for the First National Bank of Catawba County would move around downtown Hickory during its almost 100 years of existence, but for many the ongoing operation of First National represented the permanence of Hickory's institutions.

Following the Civil War families began to populate Hickory in abundance. Children were growing up on the dirt streets extending from the railroad tracks, their education becoming a concern for parents and the community. A few public schools existed in Hickory, an extension of the free school movement in North Carolina of the 1840s, but the only high school was located in Newton. The first school in Hickory Tavern was built next to the old Robinson Cemetery along First Avenue. It's structure reminiscent of the Wilson log cabin standing there now, but during the Civil War, the schoolhouse fell into disrepair.11

Overwhelmingly, a number of private schools offered instruction for students. The first was Corinth German Reformed Church. They erected a "two story building" using the upstairs for a chapel, the downstairs for classroom. Professor George W. Hahn, later author of the "Catawba

Soldier" and the Reverend M.L. Little both taught there and began a tradition of church related educational outlets. In fact, members of Corinth took the early lead on learning.

§

In the spring of 1880, Lavinia Wilfong brought together the leadership of Corinth Reformed Church in her home to discuss the idea of establishing a college, one for women, built on the model of Wellesley College in Massachusetts. "Sister" Wilfong already had the support of Henry Robinson, who donated a 22 acre tract. By the fall, Claremont Female College opened to students. For the first few years, classes were held at Corinth Church while Dolph Shuford directed construction of campus buildings. By 1883, the first building opened.

The college was a grand experiment. Sister Wilfong, with the leadership of Corinth and support from Catawba College in Newton envisioned Claremont to be a "Wellesley of the South," preparing young women for the vast social changes that were on the horizon. The leadership hoped to attract philanthropic support from the same community of donors that funded "Seven Sisters Colleges" of the northeast, of which Wellesley was a member. The money never came and Claremont was left to seek assistance more locally. Years of financial struggle marked the history of the college with a succession of leaders and teachers serving the student body.

Art, languages and strict rules of conduct were all part of the education students, both locally and from across the state received during their tenure in Hickory. Reverend A.S. Vaughan went on record to say, "a woman trained with no higher idea of her important mission on dress, to wiggle in the ball room, and to make a show in society, is indeed a pitiable example of human folly." Rules included the stipulation that "no boy over ten years old should be admitted," indicating that the college was not exclusively for just women. Young men could only visit with the written permission of parents and then for only two hours on Friday afternoon, and "no student is permitted to indulge in eating between meals." Even with these strictures, the school was an academic success, producing hundreds of graduates during its 35 years of operation.12

A host of private elementary and secondary schools also popped up in and around Hickory. Generally speaking, the reason for such was the instructors themselves. "A teacher recognized as the real master of his profession, could earn a great deal more by conducting his own school than he could teaching in a free enterprise," claimed one assessment of Hickory's early schools. Advertising their services in the local paper, educators attracted youthful pupils to come learn for a price. The Reverend Jeremiah Ingold conducted the Village and Boarding School in Hickory, teaching 12 week sessions.13 His daughter Alice began a school for girls too. Coeducational schools dotted the downtown landscape as early as 1873. Miss Mary Clute, began a "subscription school" in a "small frame building on Fourth Street and First Avenue, SW".14

Members of Hickory's Catholic Church also expressed interest in education. Like Sister Wilfong originating Claremont, Dr. B.F. Cobb lobbied members of St. Aloysius (he had recently moved to Hickory from Wilmington) to create a high school for girls, which also housed a convent.

Members of the church erected St. Joseph's Academy around the same time they built their first sanctuary, though members of the faith had been worshiping together in Hickory since during the Civil War. Run by the Sisters of Mercy, the academy operated under Catholic control for about ten years until the school was sold to the Lutheran Church. They changed the name to St. Paul's Academy. It ran for years as both a "high-class" school for boys and eventually, girls. It also aspired to become a seminary for the Lutheran denomination. St. Paul's struggled for years, around the same time Claremont Female College opened. The building and its thirteen surrounding acres were bought by Colonel Marcellus Eugene Thornton, in many ways Hickory's successor to Daniel Shuler. Thornton publicly discussed turning the campus into a hotel but the venture never went forward. It seemed that as fast as the educational outlets came to Hickory they vanished just as quickly.[15]

Northeast of town, Walter Lenoir offered a tract of land he offered to any group willing to put it to educational use. Lenoir, a Civil War veteran, had two grandfathers of significance to North Carolina's past. General William Lenoir served with merit at the Battle of King's Mountain. His home, Fort Defiance is located just north of the town that bears his name. His maternal grandfather, Waightstill Avery became North Carolina's first Attorney General. Avery also had the distinction of once dueling with Andrew Jackson. According to Ellis Boatmon, history professor at Lenoir-Rhyne College in his book on the college's history, "Lenoir offered the property in the early 1870s to several church groups, including the Lutherans of Catawba County.

Finding no takers, in 1881 he deeded in trust the 23 acre portion (of a larger 56 acre tract) to his friend J.G. Hall, a Hickory businessman, on condition that he operate a school on the site." Hall convinced Colonel H.C. Dixon, who had been teaching in Lenoir to come to Hickory. Dixon took charge of the new effort as principal, calling the school, Highland Academy.16

Leadership turned over a few times in its early years. After two years Dixon left for the job of clerk at Piedmont Wagon. His successor, Reverend T.G. Thurston, who was also pastor of Hickory's Presbyterian Church, drowned less than one year after taking the job. Next, R.K. Bryan, local newspaper editor took charge, followed by Richard Meade.17 At a point when Claremont registered 45 students, Highland claimed 32.18

In the summer of 1890, Walter Lenoir died and over the next year, J.G. Hall and a group of Hickory businessmen made a daring proposal. In March of 1891, they invited three professors from Concordia College in Conover to come to Hickory for a meeting. In the home of W.P. Huffman, the trio were offered the opportunity to take over Highland Academy and turn it into Highland College on the condition that they offer classes for the fall term. Concordia's president, Robert Yoder said yes and before the fall semester started, the new school employed six former Concordia faculty and enrolled 21 students. Perhaps the toughest to persuade was Yoder's wife, "Who did not want to leave her new home in Conover." Over the summer of 1891, "the structure was dismantled piece by piece and hauled seven miles on wagon to Hickory where it was re-erected, at a cost of $240. Even the elm shade trees were moved." According to Boatmon, Yoder joked that he would have moved the well too, if his wife had demanded it and he could have found a way.19

For its inaugural year, the school operated as Highland College. But the death of Walter Lenoir and the generous gift he bequeathed the school inspired the trustees to change the name to Lenoir College. In that first year, the school outgrew its one building, designed to accommodate 50 students. They had 113. Some instructors were forced to teach classes in their homes to alleviate the problem. Part of Lenoir's gift included an extra 33 acres that he allowed could be sold to fund the improvements necessary to the institution. Yoder drew up plans for a building to resemble that of Thomas Jefferson's plan for the University of Virginia. The two story structure housed the administration as well as classrooms and with the old Highland Academy building, the core of the campus was formed. It was known by students as "Old Main."

In those days, the college remained far enough removed from the town of Hickory proper, as to be outside the city limits. Streets took on a more informal nomenclature than they would later. In front of the college ran College Avenue, but the streets that formed the remaining three boundaries of the square-shaped campus were "Hope Avenue on the South. Faith Avenue on the west, and Charity Avenue on the North.20

The institution adhered closely to its affiliation with the Lutheran church and its benefactor. The school's second year was marked with a name change. To posthumously honor Walter Lenoir for his gift of the land upon which the campus built, the name of the school was changed to Lenoir College. The curriculum's mission as stated by the school's first catalog, was "to afford to all who seek it, a liberal culture upon Christian principles." Each day began at 8:00am with chapel. Following that classes in "Latin, German, mathematics, English language and literature, history and political economy mental and moral psychology, astronomy and natural sciences evidences of Christianity, and mechanics" filled the rest of the schedule for students.

While 1915 saw the ending of both St. Paul's Academy/Seminary and Claremont Female College, Lenoir College celebrated its 25th anniversary with an "A" rating from an inspection that spring by the Bureau of Education in Washington, DC. President of the college, Dr. Fritz said the examiner "was well pleased with our courses, teaching force, method of record keeping, our buildings, our grounds, plan of walks, driveways and building sites for new buildings, Highland Hall and equipment, society work and especially with the Yoder Memorial Science Building and its equipment. Said so many schools did not have as much as we had."21

The last decade of the nineteenth century brought esteem to Hickory as a town through many of the trappings that made a city respectable. No longer was it wayside, even though as Gus Setzer remembered when he moved to town in 1891, "there was not one foot of pavement in Hickory. The park in the middle of Union Square was then a lot where farmers hitched their horses and wagons when they came to town."22 Hickory still had a ways to go, but it was on the move. Both the Asheville Citizen-Times and the Weekly

State Chronicle of Raleigh printed multicolumn reviews of everything the town had to offer, from industry to education, with drawings of major landmarks. The Raleigh feature concluded by saying that the town "invites settlers and offers a warm welcome," while the Asheville paper ended their published tour of Hickory writing, "The hope that our lot may ever be cast in as good a place as HICKORY."[23]

1   "Catawba Leads", Newton Enterprise, March 19, 1886, p. 3.

2   Charlotte Observer, December 14, 1878, p. 2; Leslie Keller, "From Tavern to Town:

3   The Daily Review (Wilmington), March 26, 1883, p. 4; Gary R. Freeze, "The Catawbans: Crafters of a North Carolina County", Catawba County Historical Association, p. 281-2.

4   "Tough But Not Rough", Weekly State Chronicle (Raleigh), October 27, 1883, p. 1; Carolina Mountaineer (Morganton), October 31, 1883, p. 3.

5   "Narrow Gauge", Greensboro Patriot, May 25, 1871, p. 2.

6   Wilmington Morning Star, September 19, 1871, p. 2.

7   Carolina Eagle, January 11, 1872, p. 2; The Charlotte Democrat, September 16, 1873, p. 2; Lenoir Topic, July 20, 1878, p. 1; Raleigh News, September 3, 1878, p. 1; Statesville Record and Landmark, June 29, 1883, p. 2; "The Railroad Celebration at Hickory," Newton Enterprise, January 5, 1884, p. 3.

8   "State News", News and Observer (Raleigh), February 5, 1884, p. 3.

9   "Hickory Notes", News and Observer (Raleigh), November 23, 1888, p. 3.

10   "The First Financial Center", Brochure on First National Bank of Catawba County, 1974, p. 4; "First National Bank", Hickory Press, January 15, 1891, p. 5; Hickory Press, January 29, 1891, p. 5; "First National Bank", Hickory Press, July 9, 1891, p. 5. The first announcement for organization of the bank offers a different

list of investors from that of the bank's own history as it is being organized in January. J.H. Craig is listed as president and H.D. Abernethy, cashier. However, the lineup cited is noted as in place when the bank begins operation but the accompanying story refers to the last lineup as the "third attempt".

11   Carolina Watchman (advert), January 5, 1872, p. 3: "Private Schools Herald Progress", September 11, 1965, p. 12E.

12   "Girls School Noted in Day." HDR, September 11, 1965, p. 4E-6E.

13   Piedmont Press (advert), September 10, 1873, p. 3.

14   "Private Schools Herald Progress", September 11, 1965, p. 12E.

15   Hickory Democrat, January 28, 1915, p. 1.

16   Hickory Democrat, January 23, 1908, p. 5; For background on Lenoir-Rhyne, the work of Professor Ellis G. Boatmon and Jeff Norris in "Fair Star: A Centennial History of Lenoir-Rhyne College", https://archive.org/stream/ fairstarcentennioojeff/fairstarcentennioojeff_djvu.txt

17   "A Terrible Accident", Lenoir Topic, February 27, 1884, p. 3; Hickory Democrat, January 23, 1908, p. 5; Carolina Mountaineer (Morganton), March 12, 1884, p. 3; Piedmont Press, August 14, 1886, p. 1.

18   Hickory Press, November 17, 1887, p. 3.

19   "Private Schools Herald Progress, HDR, September, 11, 1965, p. 12E; https://archive.org/stream/fairstarcentennioojeff/fairstarcentennioojeff_djvu.txt

20   https://archive.org/stream/fairstarcentennioojeff/fairstarcentennioojeff_djvu.txt

21   https://archive.org/stream/fairstarcentennioojeff/fairstarcentennioojeff_djvu.txt

22   Dennis Benfield, "Hickory Resident, Nearly As Old As City, Looks Back Through Memories", HDR (Centennial Edition, Potpourri Section), June 6. 1970, p. 8.

23   Asheville Citizen-Times, March 21, 1889, p. 5; Weekly State Chronicle (Raleigh), June 7, 1889, p. 1.

An old tale exists in Hickory that once business leader George W. Hall was standing in Union Square when the train came through. He saw car after car, loaded with wood from the North Carolina mountains being transported out of the area. According to the story, Hall knew all that timber was headed for furniture factories in Grand Rapids, Michigan, home of the nation's furniture industry in the nineteenth century. He wondered, maybe aloud, if instead of that wood traveling so far north, only to have value added so it could be sold back in Hickory, at a much higher price, shouldn't the money be made locally. North Carolina trees could be turned into North Carolina furniture, if only someone would take the risk. He resolved that Hickory was the place to make such a transformation happen.[1] The story of Hall and his vision provides the best origin story on the birth of furniture as a distinctly Hickory product. As the twentieth century dawned, he would provide promotion and leadership for two companies that began a whole new industry for Hickory.

George Hall, as a young blade of Hickory, planned for a college education, not at the local Lenoir College, which his uncle J.G. Hall helped to establish, but at Davidson just north of Charlotte. In 1893 he took off to begin his collegiate career. A year later he was back in Hickory. The mercantile business of Hall Brothers, to which he was an heir, had collapsed in spectacular fashion. After the failure of a London banking firm through which George's father and uncle had been doing business, revelations spread through Hickory that Hall Brothers had accumulated debt totaling three times its worth as a company. A good portion of the bills was to Piedmont Wagon. To complicate matters, J.G. Hall was president of Piedmont Wagon at the time of the implosion. He resigned that job. He also quit as the head of Hickory Printing, the company publishing the town's newspaper, that reported the story.2

As the full extent of the collapse was becoming known, George Hall made the intrepid move to buy the retail grocery portion of Hall Brothers, and set out to run it himself. He roamed the region looking for the best fruit and vegetables for his store, advertising, "country produce a specialty." With some likely intent to rescue the family name, Hall made a success as a "wholesale and retail dealer in groceries and provisions" for the rest of the 1890s. It is likely from the vantage point of that store, George Hall stood and had his epiphany. He was still in his twenties when the thought came.3

Regionally, the idea was not new. Old Fort witnessed the first western North Carolina furniture factory in the 1870s, which moved to Morganton in the 1880s and promptly burned down. Lenoir began their own in 1889. It struggled for years and was closed more than it was open throughout the 1890s. Before Daniel Shuler's crash and burn career in Hickory, he suggested such a factory but never lived/stayed long enough to build it. Hall's vision may have come in the aftermath of such previous failures, observing the pitfalls of previous attempts in his effort to succeed in a town open to any dedicated effort. For his vision, George Hall became known as the father of furniture in Hickory.4

Turning wood into usable product was not new to Hickory, either. Piedmont Wagon had been doing it for over twenty years. A number of companies built doors and windows. In fact, Shuler used the products of Hickory Manufacturing to build his home (Harper House).5 But the idea of industrially made furniture, not building supplies was new to Hickory. Just to the east of Lenoir College, Hall and a host of investors started Hickory Furniture Company in 1901, along the railroad. Hall amassed a group of local men to contribute a capitalization of $20,000, with resources for more. Within six months after its announcement, the factory began to ship bedroom suites. The newspapers affirmed Hall's vision in front of his store, writing that "the enterprise will fill a long felt want among our wood manufacturers who have been unable to utilize to advantage the beautiful hard woods which are shipped daily from this market to other sections of the country to manufacturers of fine furniture."6

George Hall had a great influence on all furniture making that was to follow in Hickory. In less than a year, Thomas Martin of Chester, S.C. rode north on the narrow gauge railroad from his hometown to Hickory where he planned to build his own furniture factory only a few hundred yards from Hall's. Though a direct link between the two companies did not exist, there was significant coordination. They shared a side track from the Southern Railway line (formerly Western North Carolina Railroad). Also, the output of Hickory Furniture and Martin Furniture complemented each other with Hall's company specializing in bedroom suites while Martin's operation built sideboards for dining rooms.

The sawdust flew at both factories with orders from as far away as Chicago.7

At Hickory Furniture, Hall took the job of secretary/treasurer while K.C. Menzies served as president of the company. Within a few years of operation, Martin sold his interests to a group of local investors that included A.A. Shuford and Menzies. In less than a decade, they would be joined by another company, complementing the offerings of the first two manufacturers. Moving a chair factory from Surry County with a guarantee from Hickory folks of available capital at $200,000, Hickory Chair built adjacent to the other two, at what was being called the Highland Section.8 George Hall, from his musings in front of his mercantile store had created a whole new industry for Hickory, tucked away in the northeast corner of Hickory. Restoring the family name, Hall took his place among the new generation of progressive leaders whose activities became the talk of the town.

In 1904, George Hall married Ruth Ebeltoft at a home in Charlotte.9 They returned to a Hickory that allowed only limited societal opportunities for women to participate. With business activity left to men, women navigated a world of influential wives who exercised their intellect by participating in the book club of their choice. Some were very exclusive, but they offered women in Hickory a network to trade ideas on an intellectual level, as well as social jockeying for their husbands.

Ruth Ebeltoft Hall joined the "Dames of Pleasure" as a charter member in 1906. Sensing the name too risqué, the members changed the name to the Wednesday Afternoon

Book Club, a title more in keeping with their station in town. By that point, women's book clubs were well established in Hickory. The first book club in town was organized as the Hickory Book Club on November 30, 1898 with Mrs. H.D. Abernethy as its first president. Seven years later, Mrs. C.C. Bost "called a meeting of selected women to her home." There she began the "Round Dozen" Book Club (1905), which only admitted twelve members, thus the name. There followed a spate of others. There was the "Thursday Study Club" (1908), the "Do As You Please" Book Club (1910), the Cosmos Book Club (1916), the New Era Book Club (1918), and the Fortnightly Book Club (1921). These gatherings featured discussions on books, as well as occasional visits by authors. William Sidney Porter, known by his pen name 'O. Henry' came to a new club in Hickory that was named for him.10

By the era of the book clubs, a number of outlets were established for the arts in Hickory. The St. Cecilia Society was the most prominent group, offering performances to and by its own citizens. It began as a pet project of Edwina Shearn Chadwick, who came to Hickory in 1880 to teach at Claremont College. She married, moved away, but upon the early death of her husband, she came back to form the St. Cecilia Society, an outlet for those talented in music, as well as dramatics. Chadwick wanted (and got) one hundred trained voices to perform for Hickory citizens, which was quite an undertaking, considering that Hickory's population of the period numbered only a few thousand.11

The St. Cecilia Society, as well as another local group, "the Hickory Amateurs" performed for local folks regularly.

The Amateurs were the town's first community theatre group. One of their performers included a later mayor of Hickory. From the nineteenth century into the twentieth, public performance of the arts became a mainstay in Hickory. Bands remained popular entertainments too. The Catawba Station Band and the Hickory Military Opera Band played regularly, drawing crowds. In fact, on the occasion of the first street lights in Hickory, the Military Opera Band played.12

The performance home of the Hickory Military Opera Band, St. Cecilia's and the Hickory Amateurs was the Elliott Opera House. Located just west of Union Square, J.D. Elliott's theatre continued to draw crowds from surrounding towns for a variety of shows, including traveling minstrel stagings. From its opening in 1889, the grand show place was Hickory's cultural center. Then, two days before Christmas in 1902, "$30,000 worth of property went up in flames and smoke." The exact source of the fire was never determined, but the blaze became a total loss when two kegs of gunpowder from the first floor hardware store exploded. The incident, called "the most disastrous fire that Hickory has ever known," put an end to the Opera House, regarded as "one of the handsomest in the State."13

Another lavish structure, built around the same time as the Elliott Opera House and another of Daniel Shuler's projects during his short tenure, met the same fate a few years later. On a cold February morning in 1907, the Hickory Inn, the town's premier hotel caught fire, forcing several guests to jump from their third story rooms. A fuel lamp in the downstairs quarters was blamed for the incident which totaled about the same in damages as the opera house.14

Undeterred, citizens of the city vowed to rebuild. Two years later, they did. With an invitation to all "the citizens of Hickory and the general public," the Hotel Huffry opened just down the tracks from the ruins of the Hickory Inn. The name came from a mashup of the owners, Huffman and Fry and was proclaimed to be "a modern building with first class equipment."15 Slightly less grand than the Hickory Inn, the Hotel Huffry retained many of the elements of its predecessor. If it were to remain a leading industrial center with customers visiting, as well as vacationers to the town itself or as gateway to the mountains, Hickory needed the Hotel Huffry as a continued accommodation. Growing quickly in its first twenty years, by 1890, Hickory's population doubled that of Newton, the county seat. The numbers continued to rise steadily. By 1920, Hickory had grown to over 5,000.16

At the turn of the century, Hickory's most famous citizen was Marcellus Eugene Thornton. A Georgian by birth, he grew up around Civil War ravaged Atlanta and learned the trade of journalism from Henry Grady, the newspaperman who offered a renewed vision for the old Confederacy and with it coined the term, "The New South." Thornton came to town with his first wife, Elizabeth Camp Denison Rutherford Thornton. The Colonel, as he liked to be called was her third husband. She was credited with saying she married the first time for love, the second time for money and the third time for the hell of it. After John Rutherford, her second husband died, leaving his wife a considerable inheritance and no biological children, she met and married the colonel, fulfilling her marriage list.

The Thorntons arrived in Hickory around 1892, purchasing the house built by the estate of Daniel Shuler (Harper House). The couple would spend the rest of their lives in Hickory. After dabbling in coal mining in Kentucky with his wife's money, the colonel began his Hickory career as a law partner to Clinton Cilley. He soon tired of the practice and bought the Hickory Press and Carolinian, which he ran for a few years. In 1902, he bought the Hickory Electric Company, another acquisition begun by Shuler. Elizabeth Thornton, his wife, was a shareholder. Reportedly, he bought the company to wire his own home, the former Shuler estate.17 Thornton's power company tried to compete with Southern (Duke) Power until the city licensed Southern and Thornton sold what was left.18

The colonel was a man about town, in much the same mold as Shuler before him. He was into a variety of business ventures. He believed there was gold up on the Catawba River, so he started an excavation company. Occasionally, he hung out his own law shingle, serving as city attorney for a time. He started the Thornton Opera House which, with 535 seats, showed silent films as well as welcomed live acts to its stage, just as the Elliott had done before the fire. When his wife died in 1916, a prenuptial agreement left him with $50 per month, which he contested. He moved in with a "Mrs. Jarrett, a most refined, cultured lady," renaming the house "Thornton's Castle." Within a few years an ad could be read in the classifieds, the colonel looking to rent a house and remove himself from his "castle."19

To say Colonel Thornton was a colorful character only

begins to describe how his fellow Hickoryites saw him. He was once arrested by a Hickory policeman but argued so strenuously against his disorderly conduct that the officer was forced to resign.20 "The City of Hickory in Catawba County has no more interesting citizen than Colonel Thornton," was how one biographer described the man.21

Thornton even began a literary tradition in Hickory. From his coal mining experience he wrote one novel, called My Buddie and I. He incorporated his hometown into his second, though the title, The Lady of New Orleans gave no indication that Hickory was represented. Both were typical Victorian stories of finding and/or losing true love. The Times-Mercury, a Hickory paper called it "a notable contribution to contemporaneous American literature." During the summer of 1902, the book was reported to be "selling rapidly."22 Some conflict with the publisher of his second book kept, as he saw it, the work from reaching a large audience and stunted his desire to become the next great American author. Reports floated around that the colonel was planning future works, but much like his other ventures, he seemed to tire, leaving the job unfinished.

Toward the end of his career, his fortunes fading, he advertised his skills and schemes in the pages of the Hickory Daily Record. In one classified he offered the following" "Wanted - I will pay back $5,500 for the loan of $5,000 for one year. For particulars address M.E. Thornton." He also proposed to solve the automobile parking problems of 1922 "if granted a franchise." As a "consulting engineer," he offered his services to towns and auto dealers alike. His services found no takers.23

As Hickory was becoming a larger, diversified city, it soon became apparent to leaders that the job was too complex for a mayor and council, most of whom had occupational duties that commanded their attention elsewhere. In 1913, the town was one of the first in the nation (and the first in North Carolina) to adopt a charter that called for the employ of a city manager. The debate was furious at times over how much power the new position would afford a non-elected official. Former mayor, J.D. Elliott argued that "the new charter was a dangerous document." G.H. Geitner and W.A. Self argued in favor of the change during a debate at Thornton Opera House. The system of selection for city council, with wards and primaries was also part of the plan, a governmental sea change for the town, not yet fifty years old. Once Hickory adopted the new system, cities throughout the state began to look seriously at the system with most agreeing a professionalized manager marked an advance for the affairs of the city.24 Going out on a limb while most towns retained a more traditional management apparatus, Hickory leaders demonstrated their intent to see the city grow, rapidly. Their bet paid off.

As it did with its council-manager form of government, Hickory embraced new ideas and was ready to try the untried, unafraid of the future. Looking back on the town during that era, Mack A. Newton, Sr. recalled the first time he saw an airplane was in a field, somewhere adjacent to downtown Hickory. As he remembered, "the plane was tied by a heavy rope to a persimmon tree while starting the engine." To Newton, the craft "seemed to have been tied together with bailing wire. The pilot, dressed in his duster, cap and eye goggles, said a prayer with the lady who waited for his safe return, took off into the Hickory blue sky, returning a few minutes later to land near a mystified populace - anyway it was a mystery to this boy of ten years or less."25 As firsts were happening all across the nation in the new century, Hickory was right there with them, unafraid to release the old and embrace the new.

Substantial milestones were taking place in Hickory on the eve of the First World War. A new depot was built in 1912. The next year a second facility was required and Kenworth School followed Oakwood as educational outlets for the children of Hickory. The year after that workmen completed a spacious new post office building, two stories high and with impressive pilasters in front, just south of the depot.26

The town built up a new class of entrepreneurs just as it did new buildings. None came to have greater impact than George F. Ivey. The son of a Methodist circuit riding preacher, Ivey attended Duke University when it was still called Trinity College. He studied the manufacturing process with an internship in northern cotton mills, then came home, managing factories in surrounding towns before starting his own, with the help of A.A. Shuford. Ivey Cotton Mills was built west of town, in the industrial section, known as West Hickory.

Like Highland on the other end of town, these outlying communities began to create worlds of their own, as something of a challenge to Hickory proper. While Hickory itself had some manufacturing within it, the major factories bookended the city along the railroad tracks. Soon, they began to create their own districts. The need for housing and food in the areas around the factories spawned what looked like Hickory a half century earlier. For the first several decades of the twentieth century Highland and West Hickory continued to grow as satellites of the main city of Hickory, thanks to men like George Ivey.

A mechanical genius in his era, Ivey discovered the need in cotton mills for a device known as a picker stick, which helped woven cloth to exit the loom uniformly. Near his cotton mill, Ivey began building the sticks, using them for his own factory but also selling picker sticks to area mills. Now George Ivey found himself in the woodworking business. By 1911, he jumped in with both feet, deciding upon a product no one else in Hickory was making, school desks. Again, he sold to local outlets and continued development of the business he dubbed Southern Desk. The company explored a variety of products, including toys and wagon wheel hubs, but settled on any and all types of institutional furniture. Customers like Lenoir College bought classroom table and dormitory beds, while local churches lined their sanctuaries with pews from Southern Desk.27

Hickory greeted the twentieth century with as much confidence as any city in America. New industries had settled here with spectacular results. The downtown reflected the prosperity with new municipal buildings and a sprawling industrial area. Socially, Hickory offered outlets for entertainment and conversation well beyond what many visitors expected when they pulled into town. The future had no limits and increasingly, so did Hickory.

1   https://www.hickoryfurniture.com/css/1064/pdf/ProudHeritage040811.
pdf

2   Hickory Press, February 15, 1894, p. 5.

3   Hickory Press, September 14, 1893, p. 5; Hickory Press, July 19, 1894, p. 7; https://www.hickoryfurniture.com/css/1064/pdf/ProudHeritage040811.pdf; Hickory Press, December 26, 1895, p. 10.

4   Research by R. Eller in the forthcoming book on Furniture in Western North Carolina; Pamela Whitener, "Knights of Pythias Set Up in Hickory in July, 1894", HDR Centennial Edition, "Potourri", June 6, 1970, p. 9.

5   Hickory Press, May 3, 1888, p. 5.

6   Charles Preslar, "A History of Catawba County", Catawba County Historical Association, p. 486-7.

7   Charlotte News, February 6, 1902, p. 2; Charlotte News, April 27, 1904, p. 7.

8   Charlotte News, February 6, 1902; Charlotte News, October 28, 1904, p. 1; Charlotte Observer, October 14, 1911, p. 1.

9   Morning Post (Raleigh), January 29, 1904, p. 3.

10   Ned Pearson, "1st Organized In 1898", HDR Centennial Edition, "Potpourri", June 6, 1970, p.10.

11   Mary Ellen Donnelly, "St. Cecelia Music Club Active in Promoting Love of Music in Hickory," HDR Centennial Edition, June 6, 1970, Schools and Churches Section, p. 8.

12   Mary Ellen Donnelly, "St. Cecelia Music Club Active in Promoting Love of Music in Hickory," HDR Centennial Edition, June 6, 1970, Schools and Churches Section, p. 8; Pamela Whitener, "Rural Culture Mark Still Evident", HDR Centennial Edition, June 6, 1970, Potpourri Section, p. 12.

13   "Furious Flames Awaken Hickory", The North Carolinian (Raleigh), December 25, 1903, p. 1.

14   "Hickory Inn is in Ashes", Charlotte News, February 25, 1907, p. 1.

15   "Hickory's New Hotel", Charlotte Observer, September 7, 1909, p. 10.

16   https://population.us/nc/hickory/; https://en.wikipedia.org/wiki/Newton,_North_Carolina.

17   "Thornton Light & Power Co." Hickory Democrat, August 8, 1912, p. 11; Hickory Press, November 24, 1892, p. 5; Hickory Press, February 9, 1893. p. 4.

18   Times-Mercury (Hickory), January 12, 1910, p. 2.

19   "Colonel Thornton Resumes", HDR, June 15, 1916, p. 3; HDR (classified ad), October 20, 1919, p. 4.

20   "Gold Near Hickory", Hickory Press, July 13, 1893, p. 5; "A Riot in Court", Times-Mercury (Hickory), February 23, 1898, p. 1.

21   "History of North Carolina: North Carolina Biography, Volume IV", Lewis Publishing Company, , 1919, p. 159-60.

22   Times-Mercury (Hickory), January 15, 1902, p. 1; Times-Mercury, July 30, 1902, p. 8.

23   HDR (classified), February 18, 1919, p. 4; "Attention Towns, Also Auto Dealers", HDR, January 14, 1922, p. 4.

24   Greg Trevor, "Hickory Council-Manager System Is 75th", Charlotte Observer, Catawba Valley Neighbors Section, March 13, 1988, p. 6; "A Brilliant Debate on New Charter", Hickory Democrat, March 6, 1913, p. 1; "How Hickory Won For Commission", News and Observer (Raleigh), March 21, 1913, p. 5.

25   "Recalls City's Early Days", HDR, June 6, 1970, p. 5.

26   Leslie Keller, "From Tavern to Town: An Architectural History of Hickory, NC (50th Anniversary Edition)", Hickory Landmarks Society, 2017, p. 23-24.

27   "Thriving Firm, Formed in '08, Owes Much to Ambitious, Visionary Founder", HDR (Centennial Edition), June 6, 1970, Schools and Churches Section, p. 2.

The rain began on Friday night. For three straight days, it came down. By Monday morning, over 13 inches of water had fallen. After a few days, it started again, this time in torrents. Before it was over the level of the Catawba River had risen by 45 feet from its lowest level. What residents didn't know at the time was that they had endured the effects of two hurricanes sweeping through western North Carolina. The Flood of 1916 remains the largest natural disaster ever to hit Hickory. Once the rain finally subsided, "hundreds of Hickory people visited the banks of the Catawba river Sunday night and watched the wreckage float by." What they saw were bales of cotton heading downstream from the cotton mill at Rhodhiss. Hickory Brick Company, located on the banks lost 250,000 bricks. Bridges all along the Catawba were washed out. The loss of the telegraph cut folks off from news of the damage around them, which turned out to be even greater.[1]

Thanks in great part to is perch on top of Bolick's Dry Ridge, Hickory fared better than many other towns of the region. S.A. Farabee, Hickory Daily Record editor declared in the aftermath, "the Hickory spirit was triumphant today. Everybody was appalled at the great amount of damage wrought by the flood, but nobody was blue." He made a vow to his readers. "We will recover from this calamity as we have recovered from small calamities; we will build better than ever before, and will not the floods or fires stop the march forward." Calling Hickory's attitude, "the sort of spirit that builds empires," Farabee remained bullish on Hickory, less than a day after the washout finally subsided. 2

Farabee had a lot to base his optimism on, not the least of which was his position in town. Less than a year earlier, J. Carl Miller and his sister Mabel Miller Rowe took a chance that Hickory was big enough for a successful daily newspaper. Hickory had been called the "graveyard of newspapers, with the Carolina Eagle (1870), the Piedmont Press, which merged with the Western Carolinian in 1880, the short-lived daily, the Cricket (1888), and the Hickory Mercury (1891) all failing to survive. Some of those papers continued until the arrival of the Daily Record. Soon they disappeared too.3 On the fiftieth anniversary of the paper, Mabel Miller Rowe conceded the uncertainty. She, her brother and a small group "dared, in the face of considerable public doubt, to undertake what was regarded in some circles as a highly 'risky' business."4

In the first few decades of the twentieth century, the town of Hickory began to converge in ways that reflected its 'spirit,' as Farabee described it. Already a Chamber of Commerce had been organized in 1908. The new Chamber counted a total of 22 industries and 60 businesses operating in Hickory. With "growth" as its watchword, the Chamber sought to promote Hickory to greater heights, championing the new while revitalizing the old. Among their projects were bringing back the Hickory Fair which had fallen into "a state of collapse."5

One of the Chamber of Commerce directors, Watt Shuford identified a serious problem that concerned not only Hickory residents but also farmers in the surrounding county. Many were producing large quantities of eggs and milk with no real opportunity to sell their goods outside the local market. In the spring of 1910, Shuford made a progressive move. He organized a meeting where he laid out a plan for collecting cream, using the most advanced mechanical separators of the day, then turning the cream into butter and selling it for a much higher price. Watt convinced farmers to give it a try. The first month they were in business, dairymen collected enough to churn over 3000 pounds of butter. Farmers saw the price of their butterfat go up by 50 percent. As the operation hit its stride, revenue doubled. Shuford's idea guaranteed farmers an outlet for their product at prices they had never received in the past. Before long, the Creamery, located in a new brick building in downtown Hickory, began selling eggs and meat. Carloads of Catawba Creamery eggs arrived regularly in New York City.6

The "tireless energy and never failing optimism" of Watt Shuford was contagious. Certainly, Sam Farabee caught it, and so did a host of others who put their money on, and in Hickory. The women of Hickory were reading national and international stories on the women's vote movement, long before they considered the issue themselves. Their book clubs were forums for discussion of the right to vote was an issue they wanted to vocally support. During the Wednesday Afternoon Book Club (which was held on a Saturday), Mrs. J.B. Beard hosted the reading of "Angela's Business." She "gave some interesting lights and sidelights on the book, its purpose and views of the author as an enthusiastic promoter of the suffrage question." Though claiming to be an anti-suffragette, she "read some spicy and convincing arguments on both sides." Despite her views, the dining portion of the meeting was festooned with a suffragette themed table, "an effective display of the suffragette colors, in rich yellow with the contrasting black."7

Suffrage was just one of the momentous issues ladies debated in 1916. The World War, as WWI was called at the time, came just as Hickory was preparing for it. The day before Congress declared war against Germany, a local effort of men and women organized the Catawba County Chapter of the American Red Cross, based in Hickory. Early efforts included rolling bandages, serving coffee and donuts to passing troop trains, and efforts to provide first aid and water safety to the community. The chapter later expanded to include bookmobiles, blood donations and nursing services. Other than the draft board, the Red Cross became Hickory's most prominent symbol of the war effort.8

When the war came, Sam Farabee declared in the pages of his newspaper, "Hickory is Ready." Writing in reference to the fact that a camp for training elsewhere had been selected instead of ground near Hickory, the editor said, "the people here have had no intention of capitalizing its geographical and climatic advantages. But they stand ready to give as much as the nation desires." And give they did. Through the Red Cross, War Stamp drives were extremely successful. Plus, civilians adhered to conservation drives to save everything from gasoline to butter.9

By the summer of 1917, just over 500 Hickory men had been drafted. While not all of them served, all of their names were published in the Hickory Daily Record, a stipulation of the federal government.10 By the summer of 1918, reports of those killed in action started to come in. One was Hickory resident Sergeant John D. Huffman, part of the 105th Engineers, along the Rheims-Soissons salient. He was killed by a bomb dropped from German aircraft.11

Two memorials emerged from the war, one temporary, the other still seen in Hickory today. Upon the return of troops from France in 1919, the city threw a big party. After disembarking from the train, locals greeted the veterans with a scaled down replica of the "Arc de Triomphe", the huge arch in Paris. The Hickory version had the word "Welcome" emblazoned across the top. Troops received a warm reception that included a parade and a meal. Both white and black soldiers were embraced in the town's celebration, but the African-American soldiers were segregated during the festivities.12

Eight years later, when the men had returned to the jobs and a relatively quiet life, American Legion Post 48 brought a trophy of the war to downtown Hickory. A 210mm Howitzer was bought for $200 and shipped by rail to town. Dedicated on Memorial Day 1927, it was "placed here in memory the men from this community who participated in the World War."13 Over the years, city planners moved the Howitzer all around town searching for the best place to showcase its grandeur. On its anniversary of its last firing in conflict the piece of heavy artillery came back to the Union Square area for display.

The end of the war allowed the small city to get back to its purpose of growth. Richard Baker Hospital, started in 1911, closed during the war because founder and principal physician Dr. J.H. Shuford had left to serve the war effort.14

In post-war Hickory, the list grew long for the municipal improvements. "It would be an easy matter to pick out many things that Hickory needs," proclaimed A.K. Joy, secretary of the Chamber of Commerce. His list included "a new city hall, with auditorium, swimming pool, golf links, sanatorium, public park, central high school" to launch Hickory into the 1920s.15

Mayor J.D. Elliott agreed. His agenda promoted the idea that Hickory should "forge ahead." Arguing that "the time has arrived when the city of Hickory should take another move forward," he went on to say that in order "to prove to ourselves our own motto: 'Hickory does things.' we should insist that our aims be to build" a number of things, including erecting "a lasting monument to our boys who won the war" and "a city hall, auditorium and market house combined." The man, referred to as Hickory's "grand old man" would find himself in a conflict of interest when it came to the later. Already known as the builder of the Elliott Opera House and the First National Bank of Hickory, he had to decide which he wanted more, to be mayor or to construct its new city hall. The Record called on him to choose, saying, "We can depend on Mr. Elliott to do the right thing for his city."16 In the end, he chose both.

The contract for construction of a new city hall was awarded to the Elliott Building Company in early 1920 (he remained mayor until 1921). Cost for the building was just under the $125,000. In less than two years Hickory's grand new city hall was open. "Inside the walls of the building we have the City Administrative offices, the Council Chamber, Fire Department, Garage and Dormitory and two rooms for a future fire alarm system, a Police Department with a Chief's Office, a jail with a capacity for 22 prisoners, a Water Department Work and Store Room, three public toilets, a City Court Room, a rest room, and last but not least an Auditorium with a seating capacity of 1160." The city council's inventory of the building also reported that 343 lights would be on when the auditorium was in full use. For those counting, 793,000 bricks went into construction of the building.17

The early 1920s marked the 50th anniversary of the town. It turned out to be a heady time for Hickory. During construction of the municipal building a number of plans came together. First, a spate of service oriented clubs organized in 1921. In February, eighteen men joined together to create the Hickory Rotary Club. Their motto "service above self" drove them to put their shoulder to a number of much needed projects in Hickory including the paving of municipal roads and the building of a library in Hickory. The Kiwanis organized in May. They began meeting with 63 members. Their focus soon coalesced around helping underprivileged children in Hickory.18

The following year, a female counterpart to the male organizations, the Hickory Business and Professional Women's Club started. Before the decade was over, local leaders moved up to the state level and Hickory hosted the state convention.19 It was the second club for women in town. Prior to the war, 168 women got together to form the Hickory Women's Club. Mrs. J. Worth Elliott was elected as their first president and like the Rotary Club that came along later, these women had their sights set on a library building for Hickory.

The mission of the Hickory Women's Club, first know as the Community Club, was to invigorate and beautify Hickory. The group took on numerous jobs since its creation including the establishment of a "domestic science" department at Hickory High School, providing essential equipment. Their mission to encourage "the general welfare of our young people, thus encouraging good citizenship" can be seen in efforts to help open the first public library in 1922, create honors for teachers, provide scholarships and raise money tirelessly for every generation of young women coming of age in Hickory. When a plan was hatched to build a pool at Carolina Park, the Hickory Woman's club was right there, making sure the property was not sold "for business lots." In essence, they and organizations like theirs built the educational and social culture of Hickory.20

The spirit that Sam Farabee talked about brought Hickory to full flower, but a number of other organizations already met regularly in Hickory. The granddaddy of them all was the Knights of Pythias. The fraternal order organized a Hickory chapter back in 1894, some thirty years after President Abraham Lincoln suggested such an organization would be a good way to bring the nation back together following the Civil War. The list of charter members included all the local luminaries of the time, many of which went on to found later service organizations. In 1909, the United Daughters of the Confederacy honored one of their own when they named their branch the A.A. Shuford Chapter. Ruth Hall, wife of furniture maker George and Mrs. O.M. Royster, whose husband owned a retail store downtown headed the organization.21

In 1922, the UDC was joined by women seeking to recognize the American Revolution. The John Hoyle Chapter of the DAR got its name from the patriot captain of whom many of the original members claimed a connection. With reflection and appreciation of the independence of the United States a primary objective of the club, the DAR promoted education throughout the primary and secondary grades for the history education of Hickory's youth.22

Closer to the most recent war, veterans returning from Europe were quick to take up an idea started in Paris in the months following the armistice. The U.S. Congress chartered the American Legion in September of 1919 and by November Hickory established a chapter when "Major George Lyerly issued a call for local veterans to meet in the Chamber of Commerce offices, over the present Catawba Theater." Post 48 commenced with meetings in the Knights of Pythias Hall. They quickly helped spearhead the building of a pool at Carolina Park with the support of the Hickory Women's Club. A number of Legionaries involved themselves directly in the construction. The Hickory American Legion Post exemplified the vital spark of cooperation going on in Hickory by diving into an array of challenges all designed to improve life in Hickory.

The organization of clubs spread to every demographic group in Hickory, even the young. The idea of a training organization like the Boy Scouts originated during the Boer War and came to the United States after great success in Britain. John Wesley Clay, owner of Clay Printing in Hickory read about the creation of the Boy Scouts of America in

1910 and immediately organized a troop. With some claims to being the first in America, the local group took the title of "Troop 1" and began meetings regularly in the Chamber of Commerce building, downtown. A host of future leaders of Hickory would be members of that group. A prime laboratory for them was the banks of the Catawba River. They made numerous treks up and down it, where they learned everything from knot tying to camping safety.23

Over the course of the twentieth century Hickory would face a number of unseen health threats. The first serious menace came late in the epidemic wave that spread across the world, known at the time as the Spanish Flu. In the fall of 1918 cases of influenza, or 'the grippe' as it was popularly called, began to course through the American populace. Its second torrent came the following winter, paralyzing Hickory. Lenoir College counted fifty sick during the first surge, with another 150 coming down with it on the south side of town. By February of 1920, an epidemic loomed. City council members quickly acted by shutting down the city. An official ordinance imposed strict limits on mobility. Homes that had cases were required to post signs; all public gatherings were canceled including schools and churches. Fines of fifty dollars were threatened for anyone who violated the ordinance. The quarantine went on for almost four weeks and though more cases popped up after, officials boasted in the aftermath that "not a single life has been lost on the city, and all agreed that it was worth the sacrifice," referring to the shutdown.24

It took a while but slowly, activity began to percolate again in Hickory. Businesses coaxed customers back to their shops in downtown with advertisements like John Miller posted for the Hickory Amusement Company. He acknowledged the loss of business, taking it stoically but remaining hopeful. He told patrons his theatre "will be thoroughly cleaned and ventilated at once and will reopen to the public."25

Both good times and tough had greeted the folks of Hickory as it neared fifty years of existence. They had withstood wars, floods and epidemics to create for themselves a place where they could socialize, either through casual friendships or organizational union. Hickory had come a long way. Looking back from the vantage point of the early 20s was C.C. Bost, who came to Hickory fifty years earlier. He recalled only about a half dozen houses there at the time. The way he recalled it, "Hickory not only was a swaddling village, but it was deep in the mud. Hogs and cows had the right of way. A bicycle was a dream and an automobile was something of the future. This was back country sure enough, with more wood than anything else - and there was lots of liquor, almost free." Bost and his historian wife, relished their years watching Hickory grow but were equally bullish on the future, saying that "the next 10 years will be great and that under favorable conditions Hickory will gum along (ride out the bad times) on the road to prosperity."26

1   "Heaviest Rain in History Falls in This State", HDR, July 15, 1916, p. 1; "Flood Takes Immense Toll in Damage", HDR, July 17, 19196, p. 1; "Belated Flood Reports from Western Section", HDR, July 19, 19196, p. 1.

2   Sam Farabee, "The Flood Disaster (editorial)", HDR, July 17, 1916, p. 2.

3   "Hickory's Reputation Once 'Poor'", HDR Centennial Edition, June 6, 1970, Schools and Churches Section, p. 13; State Chronicle (Raleigh), March 28, 1891, p. 2.

4   Mabel Miller Rowe, "History of Hickory Daily Record Recalled by One of the Original Staff", HDR 50th Anniversary Edition, September 11, 1965, p. 2-B.

5   Jerry Spann, "C. of C. Here Has Enviable Record", HDR Centennial Edition, June 6, 1970, Unifour Section, p. 2.

6   "Catawba's Creamery", Evening Chronicle (Charlotte), July 15, 1910, p. 4.

7   "With Mrs. Beard", HDR, April 4, 1916, p. 3.

8   Anne Huffman, "Red Cross Here Since '17", HDR Centennial Edition, June 6, 1970, Unifour Section, p. 15.

9   Jordan Hensley, "100 Years Ago World War I Ended", HDR, November 11, 2018,

10   "Names of Registered In Catawba County", HDR, July 14, 1917, p. 1.

11   Salisbury Evening Post, July 30, 1918, p. 1.

12   "Hickory Arch of Triumph", HDR Centennial Edition, June 6, 1970, Unifour Section, p. 4.

13   https://docsouth.unc.edu/commland/monument/566/; Jon Goldberg, "Top Gun Ready to Roll", Charlotte Observer, December 5, 1997, Catawba Valley Neighbors Section, p. 1.

14   HDR, July 2, 1919, p. 2; Anne Huffman, "Richard Baker Founded in 1911", HDR Centennial Edition, June 6, 1970, Schools and Churches Section, p. 5.

15   A.K. Joy, "Chamber of Commerce was Active in War Work", HDR, January 1, 1919, p. 1.

16   "Hickory Should Forge Ahead Says J.D.", HDR, February 7, 1919, p. 1;

HDR, February 28, 1920, p. 4; "Hickory Past Mayors", HDR Centennial Edition, June 6, 1970, Hickory: Today, Tomorrow Section, p. 1, 10.

17   "Hickory's City Hall Contract Awarded", Greensboro Daily News, February 27, 1920, p. 13; "Open Auditorium, Thursday, Nov. 3", HDR, October 19, 1921, p. 1; "Hickory Municipal Building", HDR, November 3, 1921.

18   Anne Huffman, "Backed Many Civics Projects", HDR Centennial Edition, June 6, 1970, Potpourri Section, p. 9.

19   Gladys Barger, "Business, Professional Women of Area Look Back Over 48 Years of Activity", HDR Centennial Edition, June 6, 1970, Schools And Churches Section, p. A15.

20   Edna Cowan, "Woman's Club Organized in 1917", HDR Centennial Edition, June 6, 1970, Schools and Churches Section, p. 8.

21   Pamela Whitener, "Knights of Pythias Set Up in Hickory in July, 1894", HDR Centennial Edition, June 6, 1970, Potpourri Section, p. 9; Pearl Tomlinson, "Organization Set Up in 1909", HDR Centennial Edition, June 6, 1970, Schools and Churches Section, p. 13.

22   Mrs. Vander Linden, "Leaders Serve Community Well" HDR Centennial Edition, June 6, 1970, Schools and Churches Section, p. A4.

23   https://www.troop1hickory.org/uploads/3/8/2/0/38206189/troop_1_history.pdf

24   "An Ordinance", HDR, February 3, 1920, p. 5.

25   "Announcement" (advert), HDR, February 20, 1920, p. 2.

26   "Mr. Bost Moved to Hickory 50 Years Ago", HDR, March 4, 1919, p. 1.

Chapter 6 – "Consolidation"

From their perspective of the Roaring Twenties, Hickoryites looked both back and forward. Creating the Hickory they knew had been fifty years in the making. They were both proud and impatient, over what they had accomplished and what was to come.

In 1923, the Hickory Chamber of Commerce imagined what their city would look like twenty-five years later. The authors of the article, titled "Hickory in 1948," had no way of knowing another World War would intervene. Instead, they predicted that the city could claim both a United States Senator and an ambassador to England. By then, "a 21-story skyscraper, one of the finest in the South" would rise above the all other buildings on Bolick's Dry Ridge. The dream was ambitious. Aircraft manufacturing would be Hickory's newest industry and the town would become so large that "there is talk of taking Conover and Newton." In this fantasy of the future, Lenoir College (they did not see Rhyne coming) won national championships in both football and basketball.1

On a Friday night a few years later, at the county fair ground in Hickory, citizens took a step backward, into their own past. That night, Lenoir-Rhyne professor Pearl Setzer staged a pageant, depicting all that came before, a history of Catawba County. Her scenes included Father Time, played by Hickory City Manager R.L. Hefner, who commanded the stage and brought forth Natives and Europeans alike to populate Catawba County. It was a moment of reflection for Hickory, to look at all that had come before, and contemplate all that lay ahead.2

Father Time had witnessed a Tavern turn into a town, then a city, prosperous, active and beaming about its future. Hickory had weathered the storm of a flood and a World War, while continuing to grow substantially. With its own brand new municipal building, located just off Union Square, on 14th Street (now 3rd Street, NW), the city had a hub from which to plan and present its progress.

The 1920s was a time of new beginnings. By mid-decade Hickory sported a new high school, built on the grounds of old Claremont College, which shut down operations ten years earlier. New furniture operations added to the array of companies already established in East Hickory.3 The town was now being referred to as a "metropolis," a place that in addition to its own attractions, pointed travelers in a multitude of directions for further discovery. "The central highway from Morehead City to Asheville and the highway from Charlotte to Blowing Rock lie through Hickory," read one evaluation. The railroad line offered further possibilities. "From Hickory one can travel, without changing cars, to New York, Philadelphia, Baltimore, Washington, Richmond, Raleigh, Goldsboro, Durham, Winston-Salem, Asheville and Knoxville."4

Among the main national issues of the era was Prohibition, which proved to be a tricky business in Hickory. Forces had been at work trying to ban alcoholic beverages since the 1880s when the town's second newspaper, the Temperance Echo started calling for a ban. Since then the drumbeat grew louder. North Carolina tried to pass a Prohibition law in 1881 but failed. It tried again in 1908 to halt the sale of intoxicating liquors and succeeded with Hickory voting in the majority.5 However, loopholes existed. A number of folks in town spent $25 to get a government license to exempt themselves from the ban. Advertisements in the papers offered a mail order option from Virginia, circumventing the exclusion. By the time the federal government passed the 18th Amendment, the issue was a mostly settled matter in Hickory, except for the moonshiners. One man got 18 months "on the road" for hauling ten gallons in the aftermath of the national Prohibition.6

There were those around town who openly flouted the law. Reports of "special water" going to some of the finest homes in Hickory pervaded. At the old Shuler/Thornton house a new family, the Harpers moved in (1923) and took delivery of intoxicating spirits. In fact, on the third story of the home a makeshift "speakeasy" existed. Trusted friends were invited to come and have a cocktail. Their entry was predicated on resemblance to silhouettes posted on the upstairs wall. The practice suggests that local law enforcement looked the other way when the Harpers threw their parties. Finley Gwyn Harpers, Sr. was the town's Ford Dealer.7

The Twenties in Hickory brought some ominous trends. By then, there were more cars in Hickory than horses. While that showed progress in keeping with life throughout the nation, it spelled the beginning of the end for Piedmont Wagon. Their sales were based on a continuation of the use of horses to carry the weight of stock, especially farmers.

The automobile age threatened future sales. The spiral began just before Daniel Rhyne bought the business, putting his nephew, E.P. Rhyne in charge. He sold the company for almost six percent less than he had bought it for seven years earlier. A controversy arose at Piedmont Wagon that involved unpaid taxes during the years of the World War, even though the company supplied its product for the American army in France. By the time of the Second World War, a more mechanized campaign than the first, operations at Piedmont Wagon ceased entirely.8

With Claremont Female College gone, Lenoir College remained Hickory's only institution of higher learning. Through the Lutheran Church, with which the college was affiliated, a plea for $850,000 was made "for the needed expansion of the institution." Without funding the college struggled to grow, the lack of facilities threatening its future operations. More buildings and more land to locate them on became concerns for the administration. Years before, the college sought financial assistance from Daniel Rhyne, successful cotton mill owner from Lincoln County. He declined requests for assistance outright, preferring to require the college to develop a group of investors of which he would gladly join in. With the college needing a gymnasium and dormitory space as well as classrooms, they again came to Rhyne for money. He offered up to $300,000 with the stipulation that the name of the college be changed to Daniel Rhyne College.9

The trustees voted to accede to Rhyne's wish in order to secure the money, but alumni balked after the announcement of the name change was made. They suggested a compromise. Instead of losing its entire identity, supporters offered a hyphenated alternative, Lenoir-Rhyne College. Rhyne agreed and the name change was slated to take effect in the fall of 1925. Now the college's name reflected its two greatest contributors.10

As soon as Daniel Rhyne moved to save the college, he posed a threat to it, at least from Hickory's point of view. Interests in Gaston County which also included Rhyne, offered to relocate the campus to Gastonia, which lies to the south of Hickory and west of Charlotte. One report laid the blame at the city's feet, writing, "the proposition, according to those who know is that the town of Hickory has fallen down woefully in doing her part in raising the $600,000 endowment fund for the college." Supposedly, local backers of the college were only able to gather $30,000 toward the goal, which prompted the college to entertain the Gastonia offer. Rhyne agreed, saying, "it has come to me that some of the leading citizens in Hickory said, 'Let other places and other people put up the money and give to the college. We have the college now and it will stay here, so we need not worry about it,'" adding, "the people of Hickory have had the college a long time and have done nothing much for it."11

Lenoir-Rhyne had become something of a prize. Within Gaston County, another bid to house the college in Mt. Holly was proffered by the local Chamber of Commerce. They argued that the birthplace of Daniel Rhyne lay just north of their town and with "the National highway"and the "Piedmont and Northern Electric Railway running near by," the site was accessibly perfect for L-R's new home.12 A few days later, Lincolnton, just south of Catawba (and the county from which Catawba seceded) made a play, asserting "Lincolnton would be the logical location, this being the home of Lenoir College's greatest financial backer and friend, Mr. Daniel E. Rhyne."13 The Lincolnton paper began a campaign to raise money for the a move to their town. In all, a total of five sites were proposed as destinations for Lenoir-Rhyne, three in Gaston County.14

The fight went on all summer with Rhyne pledging $100,000 to the move, and Gastonia cotton mills extracting five dollars per worker for the fund.15 The official Gastonia bid included $265,000 to build a new campus and 100 acres of land. The college appointed a commission to evaluate all offers. The group considered a move but ultimately voted 11-2 (in a twelve hour session) to reject any move, even though remaining in Hickory gave L-R a third of the real estate they would have garnered elsewhere. The city did have to give in order to get, providing "an athletic field and show options where the trustees could obtain valuable land adjoining the campus. Hickory will back his (trustee J. Alfred Moretz's) pledge."16

Eventually, Rhyne conceded that the school that included his name would stay in Hickory by giving a massive amount of cotton mill stock to the college in the largest individual gift given up to that point. Adding $100,000 in government bonds, the gift totaled $300,000, allowing construction to begin immediately to complete Cline Gymnasium and break ground on "a thoroughly modern dormitory for the young women students of the institution."17 Once land purchases were completed, the campus consumed almost 40 acres. The most important outcome of the fight for the college was that it would continue its mission of educating students in northeast Hickory. By fall semester in 1924, Lenoir-Rhyne achieved record enrollment with its dorms overflowing, its place in Hickory assured.18

Among the many reasons to keep Lenoir-Rhyne College in Hickory was the variety of entertainment options the school provided. Chief among them were sporting contests. Baseball, football and basketball games (thus the need for Cline Gym) provided spectator sports for the community. The oldest of these was baseball, which had been played in the area since the 1880s. Lenoir College fielded its first team in 1903, the first game against Catawba College of Newton in March, but by the 1920s the city began to offer its own, semi-professional team, the Hickory Rebels. An all-around sporting extravaganza celebrated the Fourth of July in 1925 when a boxing match, swimming competitions and a baseball game between a team from Granite Falls and "Dad Sides' Rebel aggregation" was planned. Following the event, an amateur league was quickly formed. Starting that summer, a team called the Hickory Rebels began playing city based teams from surrounding towns in the Western Carolina League. The Rebels put together impressive winning streaks in both the '26 and '27. The 1927 season ended with the Rebels claiming the championship title without having won the championship game. It seems Hickory's team sported the best record for the first half of the season, tied with neighboring town Valdese in the second half but since the owners were unwilling to finance a title match, Hickory claimed victory, based on its record. After a few games in 1928, the team vanished from play with several former players showing up on other teams. The Hickory Rebels would not return to play as an organized club until 1933. 19

The growth of Hickory had been nothing short of spectacular since its first days of incorporation. But the city limits had not kept up with the expansion. The first charter allowed the boundary of the town to roam 1000 yards from the depot of the Western North Carolina Railroad. An extension took the limit to one mile, but no further. All along the rail line businesses proliferated on both sides. Quickly, two new entities emerged, Highland to the east (sometimes called East Hickory) and West Hickory. Highland incorporated into its own town in 1905, West Hickory began under the name Berryville in 1895, but changed its name to the more commonly used, and geographically accurate term West Hickory four years later.20

Both towns were industrially rich, but smaller than Hickory. When Berryville incorporated, the Hickory Press called the new community, "a very weak goblin in comparison to this city." However, the paper looked upon its neighbor to the west as "our competitor."21 The first few decades of the twentieth century saw the side towns grow, alarmingly with much of that attributable to their proximity to Hickory. Anyone wanting to refer to the three towns collectively called the span 'Greater Hickory,' which might also include Brookford (to the south of Hickory but home to a substantial cotton mill), and Longview, to the west of West Hickory. By the mid-twenties, the Chamber of Commerce included representation of all five towns. Consolidation began to emerge as a topic. 22

By late 1928, the Greater Hickory Club put forth the resolution that Hickory, West Hickory and Highland should merge. A referendum, planned for July 6, 1931, gave citizens the vote on combining the three towns into one. Most of the elected officials of Hickory voiced optimism for passage. It was the leadership of Highland and West Hickory that took a dim view of the prospect. Both towns requested a restraining order against the vote, throwing participation into turmoil. As the date grew closer, citizens from all three municipalities questioned whether the totals would be legitimate, given the injunction. They wondered if their vote would count for anything.23

Two days before the election, Superior Court judge Walter E. Moore heard arguments concerning the injunction, but did not rule. What he did was allow the voting to take place on schedule. When it did, the outcome remained sealed pending Moore's ruling. Ten days after the vote Moore ruled, dissolving the restraining order. The votes were allowed to be certified. By a majority of over a thousand votes, citizens approved the merger. Just before the referendum West Hickory dropped its objection, Highland did not, appealing to the North Carolina Supreme Court. When the decision came down in early January of 1932, Highland lost and the already announced outcome could proceed toward merger. Greater Hickory now became just Hickory. The combined population totaled more than 10,000 people.24

The 1930 census revealed that North Carolina could claim 21 cities with a population of over 10,000. Thanks to the merger, Hickory could join them.25

1   "Hickory in 1948", Charlotte Observer, January 27, 1923, p. 6.

2   "A Catawba County Event", Charlotte Observer, October 1, 1925, p. 8; "Catawba County Drifts Back Into Early Days of History With Pageant Presentation", Charlotte Observer, October 6, 1925, p. 7.

3   "Active Year Forecast By Hickory Boosters", Asheville Citizen-Times, January 4, 1923, p. 7; "New Table Factory Planned for Hickory", Charlotte Observer, January 5, 1923, p. 9.

4   J.A. Parham, "Hickory and Catawba Made Famous by Cows, Creamery and Cordage", Charlotte Observer, January 28, 1923, p. 5.

5   Hickory Democrat, February 6, 1908, p. 4; "50,000 Majority", Hickory Democrat, May 28, 1908, p. 4; https://www.ncdcr.gov/blog/2013/05/26/north-carolina-voters-approve-prohibition

6   "Government Licenses to Sell Liquor Here", Hickory Democrat, June 12, 19192, p. 1; "John Hefner Gets Eighteen Months on Liquor Count", Asheville Citizen-Times, January 1, 1921, p. 9; "Marshall & Sellers" advertisement, Times-Mercury, June 21, 1911, p. 4.

7   https://catawbahistory.org/harper-househickory-history-center; Hannah Mitchell, "Attic Art Portrays Mystery Guests", Charlotte Observer, November 18, 2001, Local & State Section, p. 13B.

8   "Daniel Rhyne Purchases Piedmont Wagon Company", Charlotte Observer, January 18, 1924,

9   "Synod Backs Appeal for College Funds", Albemarle Press, February 15, 1923, p. 1; https://www.ncpedia.org/piedmont-wagon-company

10   Boatmon, Norris, "Fair Star", p. 56-9; "Change Name of College", News & Observer (Raleigh), April 16, 1923.

11   "Gastonia Likely To Get Hickory College", News and Observer (Raleigh), May 22, 1923, p. 9.

12   "Mt. Holly After Lenoir-Rhyne College", Lincoln County News, May 24, 1923, p. 1.

13   "Lenoir-Rhyne College", Lincoln County News, May 28, 1923, p. 1.

14   "Rhyne Non-Committal As to College Location", Charlotte Observer, July 2, 1923, p. 8; "Three Offers of Attractive Sites Have Been Made Contingent Upon Removal to Gaston", Charlotte Observer, September 26, 1923, p. 14; "100 Acre Farm is Offered", Lincoln County News, September 27, 1923, p. 3.

15   "Three Offers of Attractive Sites Have Been Made Contingent Upon Removal to Gaston", Charlotte Observer, September 26, 1923, p. 14; "Gaston Secures $100,000 More", News & Observer, September 20, 1923, p. 1; "$265,000 and Sites for Lenoir College", Lincoln County News, October 15, 1923, p. 1.

16   "Hickory Pleased With Lenoir-Rhyne Decision", Lincoln County News, October 25, 1923, p. 1; "Hickory Pleased with Decision", Carolina Mountaineer and Waynesville Courier, November 1, 1923, p. 7; "Removal of Lenoir-Rhyne College To Gastonia is Now Being Sought by Commercial Body of that City", Asheville Citizen-Times, May 24, 1923, p. 1.

17   "Lenoir-Rhyne Largest Individual Gift", Lincoln County News, March 3, 1924, p. 2.

18   "Lenoir-Rhyne Trustees Buy More Land", Lincoln County News, April 7, 1924, p. 1; "Lenoir-Rhyne College Opens with Increased Enrollment", Lincoln County News, September 18, 1924, p. 5.

19   "Sports Events at Hickory's Fourth", Charlotte Observer, June 25, 1925, p. 10; "Hickory Rebels Win", Charlotte Observer, July 19, 1925, p. 15; "Organize Amateur League in the West", News & Observer, July 7, 1925, p. 10.

20   "Local Acts of the Recent Legislature", Newton Enterprise, March 10, 1905, p. 3; Hickory Press, March 7, 1895, p. 5;

21   Hickory Press, March 7, 1895, p. 5.

22   "C. of C. to Meet", Charlotte News, January 12, 1926, p. 10.

23   "Hickory People Seek Big City", Charlotte Observer, May 17, 1931, p. 7

24   "Court Orders Election Held", Asheville Citizen-Times, July 5, 1931, p. 22; News & Observer, July 17, 1931, p. 6; "Refuses to Stay Hickory Merger", News & Observer, July 19, 1931, p. 21: "West Hickory Drops Fight Upon Merger", News & Observer, August 28, 1931, p. 11; "Supreme Court Affirms Brewer Prison Sentence",

News & Observer, January 28, 1932, p. 1; "Hickory Population Found to be 10,776"

News & Observer, February 4, 1932, p. 9.

25   https://www2.census.gov/library/publications/decennial/1930/pop-
ulation-volume-3/10612982v3p2ch04.pdf, p. 351-352. Cities over 10,000 were
(in alphabetical order) Asheville, Charlotte, Concord, Durham, Elizabeth City,
Fayetteville, Gastonia, Goldsboro, Greensboro, High Point, Kinston, New Bern,
Raleigh, Rocky Mount, Salisbury, Shelby, Statesville, Thomasville, Wilmington,
Wilson, Winston-Salem.

H ickory is Cheerful." As 1932 opened in town, business leaders were describing their outlook positively concerning the national economy which was heading into its third year of the Great Depression. "A survey of the industrial situation here disclosed that more than $300,000 of new machinery and for additions to local plants, in addition to considerable investment in new business enterprises that have been started within the past few month," recounted an assessment of Hickory taking inventory of itself in the early years of the downturn.1

One manufacturer "predicting gains" among Hickory's industries was A.A. Shuford, Jr., son of the founder of Shuford Mills. At the beginning of 1932, his company produced "more twine and cordage than any other like mills in the world." After shipping over 100,000 pounds of "textile goods," he rejoiced over orders for 2.3 million pounds more. Unfortunately for Shuford, he would never see all those orders filled. In September of the same year, Shuford drowned while on vacation in Virginia Beach.2

The Hickory economy had plenty of bright spots in an otherwise bleak national picture. At the Catawba Creamery, with its headquarters in Union Square, the plan hatched twenty years earlier to consolidate the local output of dairymen across Catawba County was hitting its stride. Called "a great boon to farmers," the Creamery reported spending $350,000 for dairy products in 1931. As hard times reigned, the cooperative continued to supply butter and eggs for customers up and down the East Coast.3

But the effects of the Great Depression had visible signs in Hickory. Perhaps most engaged was the Hickory American Legion Post 48. They joined in a "war on depression" nationwide. In early 1932 they "secured 28 jobs for unemployed workmen in this community," demonstrating that the national crisis had indeed trickled down to Hickory.4

The furniture industry felt the crisis right down to its very existence. An old adage proved true that spending for furniture was the first thing cut from family budgets when money was tight and the last thing added when times were flush. The three major companies, Hickory Chair, Martin Furniture and Hickory Manufacturing, all located adjacent to each other in Highland faced a serious loss of sales. Instead of weathering the slump alone, the three pulled off a rather unique maneuver. They merged. Votes of the boards of each enterprise voted to unite their operations into one. Combined, they became Hickory Chair Manufacturing Company. One paper screamed the headline, "Hickory to Get New $1,000.000 Furniture Firm." While it was actually three companies joining forces, it still demonstrated a real commitment to the greater good. Together, the companies pooled their resources, invested in new equipment and survived the Great Depression much better than any of the three could have alone. In fact, the company innovated in its new incarnation, receiving a patent in 1938 for a new design in furniture making. It was a "supporting mechanism for upholstered chairs, settees and the like."5

Hickoryites coped with the Depression in a variety of ways. As a distraction, the city opened its civic auditorium to a variety of public events. Among the most popular were a series of boxing matches. One Monday night, 38 rounds in 5 separate matches were conducted, sponsored by the Hickory American Legion Post 48, possibly the most active civic organization during the Depression.6 Around town, square dances, ball games, concerts all continued to attract crowds and take people's minds off the bad times they were experiencing.7

Hard times hit everyone, including moonshiners. One place the Depression was being felt was in the "Hickory Booze Trade." The Charlotte News got its report from unidentified, but "informed circles" that "a pint of moonshine can be purchased for 45 cents if 'you furnish your own bottle." Brandy, which before the decline sold for up to $15 a quart was going in the spring of 1932 for $1.50.8

The Depression brought real suffering and destitution to Hickory. The county welfare department, "to relieve the unemployment situation in Hickory," hired thirty men to help "on street and sewer extension projects. Another assistance project brought a cobbler into each school to repair the shoes of children at no cost.9 Federal funds aided the loss of jobs too. Works Progress Administration money went into everything from paving streets to operation of a stone quarry in order to keep people employed.10

The biggest WPA project for Hickory came as the culmination of a 20-year dream to build a municipal airport for the city. Since 1918, hopes to build an airport northwest of the downtown area had been sought. It took the Depression and the make-work monies made available by FDR to realize an actual facility. City Manager Raymond Hefner made the project a priority, securing $200,000 to move 219,000 cubic feet of dirt to construct a 2,000-foot long runway. On May 19, 1938, the airport was christened with a flight in by Alan Jones, who flew out with a bundle of letters containing a special stamp, designated as "air mail" to commemorate the first flight out of Hickory.11 At its formal dedication, the new Hickory Airport was "pronounced by experts as one of the finest airports in western North Carolina." A crowd of 5,000 people attended.12 Officials slated that dedication for the late summer of 1940. A U.S. Senator, two governors and a host of local officials were on the agenda to be a part of the festivities that included "a program of aerial acrobatics."13

The celebration came less than a month after another devastating flood hit the area, reminiscent of the 1916 deluge. Again, with the downtown area perched on a hill, the water did not reach Union Square, but all around the damage of the 1940 Flood topped the previous disaster. One account revealed that "at Brookford and Henry River near here, the water was reported more than five feel higher than in the 1916 flood."14 The rising water cut off travel from Hickory with highways closed to both Taylorsville and Statesville, and the rail route to Morganton washed away from underneath its tracks.15

The Great Depression, the 1940 Flood and the looming circumstances of a Second World War made for grim times. But in December of 1941, the city planned for a homecoming. Lansing Hatfield was returning to Hickory. The young boy who regularly made the honor roll at the Old North School and accelerated in his musical studies at Lenoir-Rhyne College, had gone out in the world and made a substantial name for himself as an opera singer. Lauded as being "among the American top-flight singers," the bass-baritone won a performance contract at the Met in New York, just before his return to Hickory. Stories about him tell how he once worked as a traveling salesman, singing opera in his car between sales calls and that one of his instructors at L-R gave him the encouragement, and cash, to pursue his dream of trading a job selling for singing. He would go on to several leading roles on Broadway. Scheduled for a December 12th concert at the Municipal auditorium in downtown Hickory, Lansing Hatfield was expected to be the talk of the town. Unfortunately, his return was overshadowed by events taking place halfway around the world and just a few days before the show.16

Less than a week before Hatfield's concert came the attack on Pearl Harbor. Like the rest of the nation Hickory had been preparing for entry into a second world conflict by supplying recruits for the resurrected draft, enacted by Congress. In the fall of 1940, Branford Estel Few became the first Hickory draftee to begin to build the United States military for the approaching war. For a year, the number of other Hickoryites were called for service in an increasingly robust American armed forces to meet threats by both Germany and Japan.17

When the war came, the city was quick to take preventive measures. On December 8th one news source revealed that "while Hickory people, like their fellow-

Americans solemnly resolved to play their part in the grim drama of war provoked by Japanese attacks, precautions were swiftly made today to keep saboteurs away from the city's airport, water supply, communications industries and other property." The city was on alert. Airport manager John Terrell reported "the roar of war planes" passing over Hickory. "About two dozen medium boomers flew by, in three separate groups then. Aviator Al Jones (of Hickory's first airport landing fame), flying about a mile high, spotted thirty A-20 attack ships and three Navy Gruman amphibians of the Navy - all headed west, probably bound for California and the war in the Pacific."18

Hickory could already point to a number of its sons and daughters who were in the Pacific Theatre of war, even before there was an official war. D. Kelly Drum lost his brother Donald, aboard the U.S.S. West Virginia, the first battleship hit by the Japanese on that Sunday morning of December 7th. Clive Whitener's son Scott was a radio operator in the U.S. Army Air Corps in Hawaii at the time of the attack, and Minnie Seabock's grandson Walter, was aboard the U.S.S. Vega, "a navy supply ship somewhere in the Pacific."19

Drafts were soon overshadowed by enlistments as again, Hickory went to war. One volunteer used the event to change his name. Jasper Bost had gotten used to being called "Jap" as a nickname. He never liked it, but he "endured" it. Following the attack, he announced that anyone calling him by his former nickname would be "in grave danger of getting his block knocked off." Immediately, he signed up for the service, seeking to be a "flier in the war." Instead, he ended up as a sergeant, displaying his talents as a trumpeter in a GI band while stationed in New Guinea.20

Around the time of Pearl Harbor, baseball leaders put together a deal to wrench a franchise from Kannapolis, bringing the Towelers to Hickory. A team under that name had played in and around town since the 1920s when they were part of the Western Carolina League. When the league revived during the Depression, the Hickory Rebels were back.21 In 1934, they won the league championship and played the rest of the decade in a variety of affiliations, eventually ending up in the Tar Heel League. With that league folding following the 1940 season, Hickory was left without a team. Unfortunately, the victory of bringing the Towelers to Hickory as the reconstituted Rebels was short-lived. The shortage of players due to the war allowed the team to field a team only for the 1942 season. The majority of the Hickory Rebels wore a uniform of a different type by 1943.22

During its time, semi-pro baseball gained a lot of fans in Hickory. Pat Shores played, then managed the Rebels for a total of seven seasons. In his time, he recalled that there were "not too many other places to go for entertainment" and attending games was the "in thing to do," as he saw it. He also made two important points about those games. Since the Rebels played so few home games, folks from Hickory followed the team to away games. He also cited the assistance of many Hickory businessmen, who were also fans with financial support that kept the Rebels on the field. While saying investors required "proper justification for an outlay of extra funds" he admitted that they "were usually a soft touch when our ball club was in financial straits."23

As the war drew to its conclusion, Post 48 honored those who died in the war with a memorial service, presenting "Legion Gold Star citations to next of kin."24 Hickory supplied many heroic soldiers, some giving their lives in the cause. Perhaps one of the most fortunate was Corporal Johnson Huffman, who by 1943 had survived twelve battles during the first major campaign of the European Theatre, North Africa. At the Kasserine Pass, the weapons carrier he was driving "ran over a land mine" lifting the vehicle ten feet or more in the air. Other than not being able to hear for a week, he wrote his parents back in Hickory that he "didn't get a scratch" though he admitted his "hair was full of glass." In another battle, he was forced to "lie flat on the ground for at least an hour" before he could move. While there, a shell landed between him and his captain, about 15 feet away. He soon got the reputation of having more lives than a cat.25

World War II dominated the headlines of the Hickory Daily Record, but in the summer of 1944, a local event began to compete for interest. In early June, a case of polio occurred. Within a few days another case, then another. The number in and around Hickory began to pile up. Those afflicted early were sent to Charlotte, then Gastonia for treatment, but the hospitals filled to capacity and the sufferers, children mostly, were sent home. At that point, Hickory faced its worst health crisis since the Spanish Flu.

Polio epidemics were common in the United States. Since 1916, an outbreak occurred somewhere every summer. In 1935 North Carolina experienced a sweep of cases but with no coordinated system to combat the disease, the response was piecemeal. The presidency of Franklin Roosevelt changed all that. In 1938, he spearheaded the founding of the National Foundation for Infantile Paralysis. Money raised in January (FDR's birthday) provided funds to study the disease, while offering the latest treatment to victims during the summer.

Three key medical personnel took on the job of a response to Hickory's crisis. Catawba County Health Director Dr. H.C. Whims, County Health Nurse Frances Allen, and Dr. Gaither Hahn, Chairman of the local chapter of the National Foundation recognized the implications of the growing number early and formed a response. Two weeks into the epidemic they decided that cases must be treated in Hickory, but where? Dr. Glenn R. Frye at Richard Baker Hospital had accurately diagnosed cases of polio, but due to the contagiousness of the disease, had no space for those stricken.

Dr. Hahn had been in contact with the National Foundation, apprising them of the worsening situation since the first case. They responded by offering anything he needed in terms of medical equipment and expertise, but the National Foundation was not in the business of building hospitals. So Dr. Hahn, Nurse Allen and Dr. Whims looked for a facility they could occupy quickly. They settled on a camp built for underprivileged children, northwest of the city, overlooking Lake Hickory. Ordering the removal of the kids in short order, Hahn enlisted the Hickory architecture team of Mr. & Mrs. Q.E. Herman to create an emergency polio hospital.

On Thursday, June 22, at dawn, work began. Along

with employees from Herman Sipe Construction came citizens from Hickory who quietly showed up, offering their services. The mood was somber, but the work progressed through a summer shower and into the darkness. All night and all day Friday, those who went home were replaced by others who pitched in with whatever task was needed. Finally, on Saturday afternoon, the hospital was ready and received its first patient. Fifty-four hours had elapsed. The transformation was not complete but was far enough along to allow diagnosis and treatment. At first, doctors used tents supplied by the Army Corps of Engineers as local folk pounded together permanent wards.

Streets were laid out, electricity run, water and sewer lines configured, food and laundry services devised, in addition to the medical treatment of a growing number of polio sufferers that arrived hourly. Word reached surrounding states that Hickory was the place to bring children who lost the use of limbs or were unable to breathe, all dangerous symptoms of polio. The campus of the hospital was heavily guarded. Parents bringing their children had to leave them there. A few stalwart parents volunteered to cook or clean to be nearby, but most parents had to go home, not knowing if they would see their children alive again.

Meanwhile, the city had been saddled with a dubious reputation. If they couldn't avoid passing through, travelers rolled up their windows when entering Hickory. They began to refer to it as 'Polio City.' Even the families of prominent people left the city for destinations far from Hickory. However, to the parents of children diagnosed, the city was a god send. Hickory represented a miracle, ready to nurse their children back to health. The decision to establish a facility near a population of 13,000 was controversial but Hahn, Allen and Whims were adamant that a treatment center had to be established and since Hickory lay at the center of the known cases, it geographically made sense.

Despite the reservations about polio's spread, the citizens of Hickory and Catawba County poured out everything they had to assist the hospital. Farmers brought food, people continued to offer their labor to help build the facilities and staff the facility. The best example of community support came when Reverend R.B. Stroup of the Episcopal Church of the Ascension in Hickory made requests for items needed over the airways of WHKY radio and in the pages of the Hickory Daily Record. When he asked for electric fans to cool the wards, people brought them from their own houses. Those with baby beds brought them to Rev. Stroup when he identified a need for the youngest patients. Every time a call was put out for some specific item, dozens showed up and Stroup delivered them to doorsteps where waiting personnel gratefully put them to use. The national press noticed. Reporters from Life Magazine, the Chicago Tribune and other outlets followed the National Foundation to Hickory and were impressed by the partnership that had developed between the town and the hospital. They began to use the word 'miracle' in their copy.

The epidemic raged through the summer, quieted a bit in late August only to flare up again in September. Still, help came from Hickory to run the hospital and keep patients as comfortable as possible. Citizens were matched by the offerings of local businesses. For example, when downtown department store Spainhour's was asked for 50 sets of sheets, they gave 100. All around town everyone kept vigil over the number of patients and their needs. When money was needed, a group organized a fundraiser to keep operations in the black.

The City of Hickory was part of a county-wide quarantine that kept children, twelve and under from all public activities that summer. The pools were closed. So too were movie theaters. When churches were banned from conducting Sunday School, WHKY aired lessons on Sunday mornings to keep kids engaged. The epidemic occurred during the summer months when schools were out so any decision was delayed about instruction. Officials put off the new school year until cases subsided. Not since the Spanish Flu outbreak of 1920 had the streets been so deserted.

The emergency hospital remained open through the rest of 1944. Dr. Hahn envisioned the facility to ultimately be permanent, but in early 1945, a deal was struck to transfer services to Charlotte Memorial Hospital for convalescence. A caravan of cars carried 87 patients out of Hickory on March 9th with the last remaining patients, ending the story of Hickory's polio outbreak.

Already Hickory had gained the attention of the nation for its crisis, but more so for its response. When the National Foundation began its fundraising campaign, it had no better example of giving than what Hickory had done. In movie theaters across the country, a film exemplified the stellar outpouring of support, urging contributions to keep up the fight against polio. Hollywood actress Greer Garson hosted the five-minute recap of last summer's epidemic in a story titled, "The Miracle of Hickory."

During its time, the emergency hospital admitted 454 patients who were diagnosed with polio. Of that number only twelve were casualties, giving Hickory a survival rate of better than 97 percent. When compared with the previous summer's statistics from an outbreak in Chicago (with a 92 percent survival rate) the term 'miracle' seemed to fit, especially when Hickory's location was taken into account. One exception local folk took with all the national coverage was the way the city was perceived by the press corps. Situated near the Appalachians and seventy miles from a large city like Charlotte, many who came to cover the epidemic didn't expect much in the way of civilization. Characterizing everyone as farmers and hillbillies, Hickory was, at times, portrayed as a backwoods town. Even the National Foundation film shows a man in overalls bringing his stricken daughter through a pine thicket to the hospital. If the city did not completely dispel the stereotype, it challenged the rest of the nation's perception of someone from Hickory, thanks to the accurate reporting of the caring citizens provided to the hospital.

"The Miracle of Hickory" was a seminal moment for the city. Never before had the community faced such a life threatening challenge. Meeting the crisis with courage, determination, and giving solidified something about Hickory that its people already knew. Like the hickory wood that the tavern was named for, they bend, but never break. Taking a breath and reflecting on what the response had demonstrated about who they were, the people of Hickory developed a pride in their response, looking at the epidemic as both their worst and finest hour. The attention of 1944 showed the world just what it meant to be a citizen of Hickory, a member of the town, a true Hickoryite.26

1   "Hickory is Cheerful", Charlotte Observer, January 3, 1932, p. 30.

2   "Shuford Predicts Gains by Textiles", News & Observer, January 5, 1932, p. 5; "A.A. Shuford Is Drowning Victim", News & Observer, September 4, 1932, p. 2.

3   "Creamer Firm Invests Large Sum in Section", Charlotte Observer, January 10, 1932, p. 31.

4   "Hickory Legion Aids Unemployment", Charlotte News, February 29, 1932, p. 2.

5   "Hickory to Get New $1,000,000 Furniture Firm", Charlotte News, March 15, 1931, p. 9.; "Patents Given to Carolinians", Charlotte Observer, October 23, 1938, p. 11.

6   "Massey and Eller Head Hickory Card", Charlotte News, May 8, 1932, p. 13.

7   "Dance Given", Charlotte News, January 1, 1934, p. 3; "Huffman Hurls Victory, 5-3", Charlotte Observer, May 28, 1934, p. 7; "Don Richardson at Hickory", Charlotte Observer, February 25, 1933, p. 6.

8   "Depression Being Felt in Hickory Booze Trade", Charlotte News, March 27, 1932, p. 23.

9   "Job Relief Plans Are Formed", Charlotte News, November 13, 1932, p. 5.

10   "Brings Total Jobs Approved Up to $466,730", Charlotte Observer, September 20, 1935, p. 17.

11   Charles B. Pegram, "Airport Idea Born in 1918", HDR, June 6, 1970 Centennial Edition, Early History A-13.

12   "Hickory Plans for Big Event", Charlotte Observer, September 6, 1940, p. 11; "Hickory Crowd Hears Senator", Charlotte Observer, September 8, 1940, p. 8.

13   "Hickory to Dedicate New Airport Today", News & Observer, September 7, 1940, p. 7.

14   "Hickory Region Has Extensive Damage", Charlotte Observer, August 15, 1940, p. 2.

15   "Workmen Busy Clearing Debris From Highways", Charlotte Observer, August 15, 1940, p. 16; "Floods", News & Observer, August 17, 1940, p. 5; "Flood Damages Burke", August 15, 1940, p. 13.

16   "Hatfield Has Enjoyed Rapid Rise to Fame", Charlotte News, October 23, 1941, p. 12; "Lansing Hatfield Wins 'Met" Contract", Rocky Mount Telegram, March 27, 1941, p. 3; "Hickory Artist Sings Sunday", Charlotte News, March 1, 1941, p. 10; "Singer Dies in Asheville", News & Observer, August 24, 1954, p. 5.

17   Charlotte Observer, October 30, 1940, p. 20.

18   "Precautions Invoked by Town of Hickory", December 9, 1941, p. 11.

19   "Men Of Hickory Area in Pacific War Zone", News & Observer, December 11, 1941, p. 16.

20   "Hickory Youth Has Discarded Name 'Jap'", Statesville Record & Landmark, December 11, 1941, p. 4; "Yank Club in New Guinea", Brooklyn Citizen, July 20, 1944, p. 5.

21   "Conover Trips Rebels, 7 to 5", Charlotte Observer, June 23, 1933, p. 17.

22   "Congratulation To Hickory Rebels; Poor Finish Fails to Dim Luster of Tourney", Charlotte Observer, September 12, 1934, p. 16; "Hickory Takes Over Kannapolis Franchise", Statesville Daily Record, December 24, 1941, p. 4.

23   R.M. (Pat) Shores, "Just Like It Was", Carlton Press, NY, 1975, p. 74-5; https://lrbears.com/hof.aspx?hof=106

24   "Will Honor War Dead", Charlotte Observer, May 25, 1945, p. 28.

25   "Veteran Of Dozen Battles Has More Lives Than a Cat", Charlotte Observer, July 1, 1943, p. 7.

26   For background on the 1944 Polio Epidemic in Hickory see "Polio, Pitchforks, and Perseverance: How a North Carolina County Named Catawba Built a 'Miracle'", Redhawk Publications, 2017, p. 160-345.

In 1951, the streets of Hickory changed. In the years after the merger of Hickory, West Hickory and Highland, a unified street numbering system had been discussed. Almost twenty years later, the city took the step, hiring UNC professor John Parker to rename every street. His plan was adopted unanimously by Aldermen. "The new system used the intersection of the Southern Railway and a main north-south street as a center to divide the city into quadrants with numbers running outward from it. Street addresses will carry with them the notation 'NE' 'NW' 'SE' 'SW' depending on the quadrant in which the point is located."1

The system created a entirely new city. Originally, the downtown area included streets like Watauga Avenue and Atwood Street. After one observation of "'Mud! Mud! Mud!' is the name of all the streets in Hickory," a campaign began to improve the downtown thoroughfares, along with a numbering system for their identification. City officials made the first change in 1907. Watauga Street became 14th Street in the early twentieth century incarnation. At that point, the precedent of naming east/west routes as avenues and north/south as streets became set as part of Hickory's nomenclature. Also, the name of the downtown row of stores facing the railroad tracks to the south was officially changed to Union Square. Previously, it has been known as Park Place. That name became the designation for the area south of the tracks. Suggested by a Mr. Calvert at the

Post Office, the streets took on the feel of a larger city. But the new designation paled in comparison to the sweeping changes of 1951.2

The grid imposed the use of words like 'circle,' 'drive,' and 'court' to designate thoroughfares that meander or spring from the main roads. While sensible in its time, over the years there have been spoofs, arguments and studies of the street system in Hickory with some citizens perplexed, others infuriated by the complicated design. Called "engineering madness" by one citizen, former city planning director Tom Carr contended that "there is some logic behind it, even if it doesn't appear that way on the surface."3 The renaming of Hickory's streets revealed a growing urbanism following the nervous period of World War II and the polio epidemic.

The same year as the emergency hospital came a new organization that very much announced the arrival of the city made its debut. In late 1943 citizens celebrated American Art Week in Hickory. Interest generated by the event prompted Paul Whitener, an artist himself, to propose organizing a permanent organization, the Hickory Museum of Art. "The first small-city art museum in North Carolina" opened to great acclaim with a dedication keynoted by a former governor. From the beginning the museum displayed pieces from some of the "outstanding artists of America." One early assessment of the museum called it "one of the lustiest infants in the world or art." The characterization went on to say that the HMA "has completely skipped the toddler stage and is already taking vigorous steps."4

The Hickory Museum of Art indicated that the city had

arrived as a center for culture. Just as Hickory became a hub of business with its various industries of a half century earlier, the new museum offered another reason to regard the city as important. In fact, it was the deciding factor for an industrial giant to relocate to Hickory in the 1950s. When General Electric sought to build a "20 million dollar distribution transformer plant" in 1955 at the site where Hickory, Conover, and Newton meet, the establishment of the HMA was one of those cultural oases that impressed GE officials. The fact that such a small city contained such an ambitious museum sent such a strong message of vibrancy. It helped sway the choice of location.5

Organizations like the Hickory Museum of Art gave the city stature. Along with the publicity of the polio epidemic, the rest of the nation began to hear about a multitude of activities going on in Hickory, giving it a reputation that extended well beyond its place as a regional hub. Unlike other small cities of comparable size throughout the South, Hickory began to walk the tightrope line between friendly small town and the developing economic nerve center of western North Carolina.

The downtown area burgeoned with merchants, many located along Union Square, some of these stores spanning multiple generations. Perhaps the best examples of a business handed down from father to sons was the clothing retailer Zerden's. I.E. Zerden opened the doors of the haberdashery, called "The Underselling Store," in 1908 in the Killian Building. Eventually, he would house his company in his own building, expanding his offerings to include clothing for the entire family. As his own family increased, his children too worked in the store as they grew up. This tradition led to son Marvin, after returning from the service, joining the company and eventually assuming the role of managing things. As he once conceded, "I was expected to (run the store)." The next generation expanded Zerden family stores in Hickory as Marvin's brother Howard opened Colony Casuals. The success of the Zerden family along Union Square represented the growth of Hickory itself, benefiting all who bet on the future. "I'm the gambler in the family," Marvin once said. He gambled on business and he gambled on people.

The Zerden family broke quite a number of barriers in Hickory. Besides becoming one of the first successful Jewish merchants in town, the family was also pioneers of civil rights. One Ridgeview resident pointed out that the Zerden stores (including Colony Casuals) were retailers where African-Americans were welcome to trade without worry in a still largely segregated downtown. "If you went to their stores, you felt comfortable," says Margaret Pope. "They were very friendly and accepting. They would have no problem starting us a charge account."

In 1948, a second radio station hit the airwaves around town. WIRC began broadcasting as an independent (meaning no network affiliation) AM station. Prior to the war, WHKY went on the air, using the Hotel Hickory, the city's tallest building for its tower site. In fact, WHKY built studios as an annex of the hotel. One story purports that founder Ed Long used a mule and plow in his quest to pull together scarce radio parts so that he could begin transmitting a signal in 1940. It was WHKY that offered crucial programming during the summer of 1944 to quarantined children and adults alike. The new radio station snagged a former WBT production manager, Harry Shook as its station manager to offer Hickory an alternative listening experience.

The maturation of Hickory in the post-war period brought many of the features of cities much larger in population. Throughout the 1950s, WHKY and WIRC competed as crosstown rivals, with WHKY moving for a time to the old Elliott-Carnegie Library space. By the 1960s, both had added an FM component, though the band had yet to gain popularity. With the coming of "rock'n'roll" as a viable musical force in American life, WSPF signed on in October 1963, launching to the sounds of the Beach Boys, "Little" Stevie Wonder and Dion. The radio market demonstrated a real diversity, supported by constituents within. By the end of the 1960s Hickory would also be home to a television outlet, when the Long family, originators of the first radio station in Hickory, signed on WHKY-TV, a UHF channel 14.6

Hickory saw explosive growth from the fringes of town, too. Since the 1880s a small outer city community developed north of the center city along what would become Highway 127. Passing just east of Union Square, the road headed in a north/south direction, in front of Dolph Shuford's home of Maple Grove with its adjoining farm, following the hills up and down as the road headed toward the Catawba River and Alexander County beyond. It was originally called Windy City.

Opinions vary on the origin of the name. Some pointed to the plain upon which the area rose and the breezes it brought. Others likened it to a relationship like that of Chicago to Hickory's New York. But many, including residents were willing to admit, the moniker came from the expansive talk that came from everyone there. In 1912, the Hickory Democrat published a column about what was going among residents with the heading of "Windy City Breezes."7 It didn't take long before a new, more flattering name was in order, though for many, the old name stuck.8

By the end of the 1920s, the community's school outpaced all others in Catawba County for growth in attendance, a sign of growth in the area. It was called Viewmont School and slowly the community began to adopt the name. Like the Nile River in Egypt, commerce in Viewmont hung closely to the corridor of Highway 127. Behind those buildings on either side stood the homes in neighborhoods with people who would support those businesses. As 127 grew, eventually to five lanes, so did the commercial district along it, taking shape along as a bit of a city within a city, presenting a distinct personality all of its own.9

Among the residential sections of Hickory, neighborhoods began springing up as houses were built. Oakwood developed adjacent to the cemetery of the same name as well as the school that would soon take the name also. On the southeastern side, Kenworth School spawned more than an accidental conglomerate of houses. In the interest of growth, the Kenworth neighborhood came into being as the city's first planned subdivision. Bullish that "no such development has ever been undertaken in Hickory before," builders laid out streets for an orderly and fashionable neighborhood, hoping "the people of Hickory appreciate the magnitude and cost of this undertaking for the building up and development of our city as well as beautifying its suburbs." Green Park also dated its neighborhood around the school that ultimately became headquarters for the Hickory Public School system. The area known as Mountain View was likewise named for an elementary school located in its midst in the shadow of Baker's Mountain. Portions of the community were later annexed by the city.10

Viewmont and Kenworth were not the only unique sections surrounding Hickory. Directly across the tracks from Union Square, the African-American section of town developed. As late as the 1870s the area included families, both black and white but with the Jim Crow era, covenants on housing elsewhere in town, compacted folks into two African-American neighborhoods, Ridgeview and East Hickory. The larger of the two areas, Ridgeview was known for a while as Bobtown, a tribute to one of its early black residents, Bob Simonton.11 It wasn't until a school was established, much like Viewmont, that the community took on the new name of Ridgeview.12

The Ridgeview neighborhood became a community that often looked to itself for support and commerce. Grocery stores, restaurants, doctor's offices and even a theater were built in its small but thriving business district. However, the real center of Ridgeview was its school. Accredited in 1928, it went on to build a stellar reputation in several areas. At one time the highest level of credentials by a faculty belonged to Ridgeview High School. In addition to its academics were an outstanding band. But the school gained the most acclaim outside the community for its sports programs, especially football.

In the era of segregated schools, perhaps the most interracial event in Hickory were Friday night football games in the fall, when the Panthers were playing. Starting in 1957, successive teams went undefeated in the regular season until integration brought an end to the high school in 1966. During that time, teams won a total of 74 straight games, a record never bettered in North Carolina high school competition. But one team stood above the other excellent teams for its performance in 1964. They were called the "Untouchables."

After losing the state championship, team members came back from the 1963 season prepared to work even harder to achieve their dream of going all the way. Their coach, Samuel W. Davis, Senior espoused a philosophy he drilled into players at every opportunity, "kill a gnat with a sledge hammer." He designed his defense to show no mercy. Along with assistant coach Roger Scales, an offensive genius, the two plotted a strategy for the 1964 season that would surprise even them.

At the beginning of season, Coach Davis expressed doubt as to the team's potential, calling his 64 squad "weak." One of the group of seniors who played both sides of the ball (most starters did) said, "I think Coach said that to keep us humble. After losing the previous year, he wanted us to stay focused." As the season progressed, members began to notice that they had shutout every opponent. About midway, some began to think of playing a season in which no opponent scored on them. Coach Davis cautioned against such a goal, saying they should instead focus on winning the state championship. A few years earlier the team almost pulled it off, shutting out every team until they got to the big game where they lost. The coaching staff did not want a repeat. When the earlier team was on its winning streak, they too were dubbed "The Untouchables" until the defeat when announcer Ellis Johnson was reported to have remarked, "they have now been touched." The name "Untouchables" came from a popular television show of the era and as the season progressed with games totaling 52-0, 40-0 and the like, pressure mounted.

The game that decided the Northwestern Conference championship was played at Newton against the Central High Hornets. The contest was never close. Ridgeview walked away with a 36-0 victory and rolled into the playoffs ready for any team. The newspaper headline said it all, "Ridgeview Explodes Again, Defense Still Unscored On," assuring the team a shot at the state championship.13

Because of interest which might partially have been to see if the Untouchables could stay that way, the big game was played at Lenoir-Rhyne College. One memory for team members was the grass they were about to play on beat anything on their home field. At Ridgeview, the gridiron was extremely gritty. With only dirt to cushion any tackle, everyone called their home field 'the dust bowl.' One player laughed that if you saw a dust cloud over Hickory on a Friday night, you knew Ridgeview was playing ball. The championship game remained tense during the first half. Opponent Hamlet fought to Ridgeview's five-yard line.

Guard Xenophone "Jobo" Lutz, in an excited moment yelled to the other team, "You're not gonna score." Team captain John Hodge stopped him by saying "Shut up and play some ball." The Panthers held off their opponents until halftime.

In the second half, the Untouchables put the touch on Hamlet for two scores and a pair of two-point conversions to claim the "North Carolina Negro Class AA Championship." Maybe just as importantly, they attained their title by scoring 446 points that season, allowing their rivals not one point. Zero. Quarterback Allen Pope said that some teams considered it a victory to just want to score one touchdown on them. No team ever did in 1964.

The accomplishment of the Untouchables remained well-known in the Ridgeview community, but in the wider world of Hickory, integration and the turmoil created by it shelved the popularity of the team's feat. Few teams in history have played such a complete and perfect a season as did the 1964 team. Even the first combined race team at Hickory High in 1966 that went on to win the state championship itself never dominated teams the way that Ridgeview contingent did. In 2018, the United Arts Council of Catawba County heard the story and successfully won a grant to build a work of public art to honor the team. After extensive discussion among the citizens of Ridgeview, an arch was constructed to celebrate both the team and the high school whose banner they carried. The site for the arched monument was the 'dust bowl' where the team played their home games.14

Sports like football were popular in Hickory, but so were a variety of other activities. From a sporting perspective one venue that clearly defined Hickory as an important location was Hickory Motor Speedway. Opened in 1951 as a dirt track, the venue attracted NASCAR's premier circuit, the Grand National Series within two years. For two decades the track welcomed drivers like Junior Johnson, who won seven races there, and Ralph Earnhardt, as well as local talent who rose to the top of the profession, like Ned Jarrett and Bobby Isaac. Until NASCAR began to pursue larger tracks for its premier series, drivers brought their cars to race regularly on the 4/10s mile oval, earning Hickory Motor Speedway, which is currently within the town limits of Newton, the slogan, "The World's Most Famous Short Track" and "Birthplace of the NASCAR Stars." After the Grand National circuit left in 1972, the track held fewer NASCAR events, while still dropping the flag on local drivers every weekend from spring to fall.15

The location of the Hickory Motor Speedway, along Highway 64/70 represented a major change for Hickory after about 1960. The "bypass" as it was called, contained both U.S. Highways 64 and 70 and ran in an east/west direction, south of the downtown district. With the exploding popularity of personal automobiles in the post-WWII era, the 64/70 strip served a dual purpose. First, it provided another commercial district to Hickory. Discount stores like Sky City and W.T. Grant's came along with gas stations and restaurants, then malls. In March of 1966, developers broke ground for Catawba Mall, a 23 acre site that would accommodate 2,000 cars and a shopping space of 275,000 square feet. Several major downtown retailers left their stores in and around Union Square for Hickory's new center of commerce. Belk's, J.C. Penney's and eventually regional chain Spainhour's all set up shop in the "all-enclosed shopping center."16

Development continued so rapidly that ten years later a second, grander mall broke ground down the highway from Catawba Mall. Many of the retailers who moved to the bypass once took the further leap to become a part of Valley Hills Mall, a venue with almost twice the floor space of its predecessor. Where the mall went, so did other businesses, creating a shopping experience reminiscent of the days when everyone came to Union Square to look and buy, but now with strolls from store to store in climate controlled comfort.17

The other purpose served by the 64/70 Bypass was its use as a detour for the yet-to-be-built Interstate 40. The federal highway system began construction of Interstate 40 in the late 1950s, but a major portion of the road through Catawba County went unfinished until the mid-1970s. The delay turned out to be both a blessing and a curse to Hickory. During that fourteen-year period, interstate traffic on the bypass was fierce, some called it "nightmare alley because of the frequent wrecks and heavy traffic." While the problem meant frustration for customers, it meant more customers for those businesses.18

One of the pioneers along 64/70 was Leroy Lail. In 1963, he took over management of a wholesale furniture showroom, part of a complex his father-in-law had developed, along with a restaurant and motel. Having become a center of furniture production, Hickory became a destination for buyers. In the early 1950s, manufacturers began to pool their resources to create a semi-annual showroom space for furniture buyers to see new lines and make purchases for their stores. By 1963, a building strictly for that purpose went up along Highway 321 in the northwestern corner of the rapidly expanding city. It was called the Hickory Home Furnishings Mart, containing 86,000 square feet of display space. But Leroy Lail had a different idea. Catering to manufacturers, some out of the area, who also wanted to get their products in front of buyers, he put his resources into his own showroom, calling it the Hickory Furniture Mart. With only 12,000 square feet at the start, he offered buyers things the Home Furnishings Mart could not, including flexible hours, a diversified array of furniture and accommodations at Mull's Motel and Restaurant.

The Hickory Furniture Mart gave buyers another place to go when in town along the 64/70 strip. Every six months after the conclusion of one furniture market, Lail would begin construction on an addition, finishing it just in time for the next gathering. When he expanded the Furniture Mart it was nowhere near the city limits of Hickory. He remembers building sewer lines for his complex to serve customers at the motel, in hopes of attracting the city someday. Within a few years Hickory did, first placing much of the burgeoning development of the 64/70 corridor in the Hickory Planning District, then annexing the area outright. By that point Leroy Lail had much greater plans for the strip.

Seeking to offer his customers, which were then still furniture buyers, a luxurious stay while in Hickory, he sought a franchise with the prestigious national chain, Holiday Inn. With land at the end of Lenoir-Rhyne Boulevard, he had the perfect location with easy access to the just completed Interstate 40. Initially, he was turned down. One had already been established next to Catawba Mall. But following one of his business axioms that helped him grow in the business world, "if at first you don't succeed, try, try again" he kept at it until an opportunity opened up. In 1985, he cut the ribbon on the Holiday Inn at Crown Plaza, one of the most stylish in the Holiday Inn group. The Hickory Furniture Mart and the Crown Plaza bookend Valley Hills Mall along Highway 70 (64 had since been re-designated elsewhere).

The semi-annual furniture market in Hickory had been a fixture of the local economy for twenty years. The entire town geared up to welcome, entertain and sell out of town buyers on the output of a growing number of factories in and around town. But in 1984, the market changed. Hickory had always competed with High Point for supremacy in the wholesale furniture arena. By the early 80s even Hickory companies began to promote their wares in High Point, abandoning showrooms at both the Hickory Home Furnishings Mart and Leroy Lail's Hickory Furniture Mart. A crisis loomed.

With the loss of the April and October furniture markets, the Hickory economy would be impacted negatively. Both marts adapted in different ways. The Home Furnishing building on Highway 321 closed but later found a new life as the headquarters for a worldwide producer of fiber optic cable, Siecor. Lail continued the Hickory Furniture Market, but as a retail, not wholesale operation. The 800,000 square foot facility welcomes customers ready to furnish their home with furniture year round. In 2020, the Mart, with display areas on three floors, celebrated sixty years of continuous operation.19

The post-World War II years had been flush for the furniture makers in Hickory. New companies sprang up regularly, looking to make a name for themselves while supplying the market with distinctive pieces. The furniture business was mostly the domain of men, especially in management. As Leroy Lail once observed, more furniture companies got started over a drink than anywhere else. The 1960s saw an anomaly when Nelle Burns not only rose to the top of a company, she managed to sell the output of her factory to the most prestigious house in America.

Cox Manufacturing started in 1933, with Nelle Burns as an assistant to owner William Cox. When he died in 1952, the future of the company looked uncertain. Nelle and her sister Frankie Burns bought the company. She not only kept pieces rolling off the assembly line, she also managed to attract the attention of not one, but two First Ladies of the United States. Both Mamie Eisenhower and Claudia "Lady Bird" Johnson bought furniture to be used in the White House during the administrations of the husbands as president. She never changed the name of the company as a tribute to her one-time boss but during her tenure she quadrupled the output of Cox Manufacturing, proving that the furniture business was not a boys only club.20

Manufacturers like Cox, Century Furniture, and a whole host of other producers had turned the industrial art of furniture making into an institution in Hickory. By the late 1950s, companies were looking for help to train their workforce in developing technologies. So were other companies around the city, making other products. The problem was not unique to Hickory. Producers all across North Carolina echoed the problem. In 1958, Catawba County embarked on creating an industrial education center, located just beyond Leroy Lail's Hickory Furniture Mart, as did other centers of commerce across the state.

County commissioners selected Robert Paap, a Michigander to build the educational facility. He went to work constructing a half million dollar building, with another million's worth of equipment inside. The center was one of nine chartered in the state and when North Carolina began its community college system, the Hickory site got wrapped up in the new arrangement. For a while it became Catawba Valley Technical Institute, then a technical college before changing in 1988 to Catawba Valley Community College. Paap remained president all the way until the final name change, longer than any other leader in the system. His message was the same for all of his 28 years as head of the college, saying "no course of study is of value if it does not benefit commerce and industry as well as the students." 21

By the time Hickory reached its centennial, growth had reached such a level as to diversify the city widely. Many of the modern institutions embraced by Americans in the 50s and 60s came to Hickory in abundance. The baby boomers were growing up in neighborhoods all across Hickory, filling schools and colleges that had a range of options for them as they grew up into adults and began to raise their own families.

1   "Hickory Getting Signs" Charlotte Observer, May 24, 1951, p. 2; "New Numbering Plan", Daily Times-News (Burlington), October 4, 1950, p. 5; "New System" News & Observer, October 5, 1950, p. 23; Kathryn Wellin, "How Hickory Arrived at Its Confusing Streets", Charlotte Observer, November 24, 2002, Catawba Valley Neighbors Section, p. 1,3.

2   Hickory Press, January 17, 1895, p. 8; Hickory Democrat, February 13, 1908, p. 3; "Names of Streets to be Changed and All Streets and Houses Numbered", Hickory Democrat, October 3, 1907, p. 6.

3   John Heckinger, "Hickory Streets 'Madness'", Charlotte Observer, October 18, 1989, p. 20B; Kathryn Wellin, "How Hickory Arrived at Its Confusing Streets", Charlotte Observer, November 24, 2002, Catawba Valley Neighbors Section, p. 3.

4   "Hoey to Open Art Museum", Charlotte News, February 4, 1944, p. 14; "Hickory Museum of Art Off To Fine Beginning", Charlotte Observer, September 24, 1944, p. 42;

5   Emery Wister, "New Installation to Employ 1,100", Charlotte News, January 7, 1955, p. 1; State Will Get New GE Plant", Rocky Mount Telegram, January 7, 1955, p. 1; Dr. Gary Freeze. "The Catawbans: Volume 3, Boomers and Bypasses", 2016 Catawba County, NC, p. 20

6   https://files.nc.gov/ncdcr/nr/CT0177.pdf; Bill Chapman, "WSPF Signs Off In Hickory", Charlotte Observer, December 31, 1987, p. 2C; https://en.wikipedia.org/wiki/WHKY-TV

7   Times-Mercury, April 3, 1912, p. 2; "Windy City Breezes", Hickory Democrat, October 31, 1912, p. 6.

8   "Two Windy City Stores Consolidate", Charlotte News, August 16, 1947, p. 9.

9   "Attendance at School Record", Charlotte News, May 8, 1929, p. 5.

10   "The Kenworth News", Hickory Democrat, December 13, 1913, p. 4; "Greater Hickory", Hickory Democrat, February 19, 1914, p. 3.

11   Lenoir Topic, October 19, 1887, p. 3; Dr. Gary Freeze, "The Catawbans,

Volume 2, Pioneers in Progress", Catawba County Historical Association, p. 38.

12   "Booker Head of Ridgeview High", Charlotte Observer, November 20, 1932, p. 53.

13   "Panthers Net Championship", HDR, November 7, 1964, p. 10; "Ridgeview Explodes Again, Defense Still Unscored On", HDR, November 21, 1964, p. 10.

14   "The Untouchables: The 1964 Perfect Season of the Ridgeview Football Panthers", documentary, 2020, Catawba Valley Community College, A Redhawk Publications/HandsOnHistory Production.

15   https://hickorymotorspeedway.com/about.php

16   "Work Started for Catawba Mall", Charlotte Observer, March 27, 1966, p. 26.

17   "Dinner, Dancing Down at the Shopping Mall", Charlotte Observer, May 10, 1978, p. 9.

18   "Hickory By-Pass on I-40 To Be Opened Dec. 1" Asheville Citizen-Times, September 4, 1975, p. 29.

19   Leroy Lail, "Win-Win", Redhawk Publications, 2020.

20   "Cox Company in Hickory Is Purchased", Charlotte Observer, June 20, 1952, p. 6; "Hickory Firm Handles Order For Eisenhower", Charlotte Observer, February 11, 1954, p. 8.

21   "Local Students Can Attend Center", Statesville Record and Landmark, August 19, 1960, p. 1; Karen Barber, "Opportunity Extended CVTC President's Stay", Charlotte Observer, Catawba Valley Neighbors Section, p. 1; "Sign Makes it Official: CVTC is Now CVCC", Charlotte Observer, January 27, 1988, Catawba Valley Neighbors Section, p. 3; "CVCC to Inaugurate 2nd President in School's 28-Year-Existence", Charlotte Observer, November 30, 1988, Catawba Valley Neighbors Section, p. 13; Larry Penley, "Catawba Valley Created To Fill Widespread Needs", Charlotte Observer, January 23, 1967, p. 27D.

The celebration of Hickory's centennial was unlike any party the city had ever seen. Throughout the year of 1970, events were staged to herald Hickory's history as a means to propel it forward another one hundred years. One old idea that became new again was the beard. Most of Hickory's founding fathers wore them. The new crop pledged facial hair to each other again, creating a "Brothers of the Beard" society. Those that insisted on remaining clean shaven paid fines. Badges showing membership in the club were sold for one dollar each as just one of many fundraising avenues to finance a lavish party.1

For ten days in June, citizens saluted their past. "Hickory is going to pause - to withdraw from the maddening pace of the 20th century life - and take a nostalgic look at the frontier village that once existed in the pine-studded western Piedmont," was how the commemoration was described. Governor Bob Scott came and cut a birthday cake. Merchants joined in with window displays reminiscent of their 19th century counterparts, complete with wardrobe and pricing. "The list of attractions and events goes on and on - races, music, a carnival, a performance by the U.S. Air Force's Thunderbirds, sporting events and many others" reminded Hickoryites of where they came from as they bounded with great energy into the future.2

By the summer of 1970, Hickory had a sense of its prominence in the world. Three years earlier, officials from the city pitched their advantages in front of a committee in Milwaukee, Wisconsin, seeking to be called an "All-America City." Of the 116 who vied for the title, eleven won including Hickory. Red, white and blue banners festooned Union Square as soon as the news was announced. Citing the city's stance as "a pioneer in interracial relations" the application touted a litany of accomplishments including an "expanded airport," "a new sewage treatment plant, a new community hospital, a community theater, a ballet company and a symphony orchestra."

Over the years, business and municipal leaders gave Hickory a number of nicknames, including "Hickory Hums" and a title bestowed upon it by "the head of a large eastern transportation system" in the 1930s, "Best-Balanced City" which showed up on the front license plates of cars all around town for decades. Now it boasted the banner it just won, "All America City." Hickory would again vie for the right to renew its claim itself in 1987 and 2007, receiving the award both times.3

One of the assertions made by representatives of Hickory the All-America City committee was the progressive state of race relations in the city. After winning the award that bond deteriorated to the point where Mayor Julian Whitener declared that a "state of emergency" existed. When Hickory High was integrated in the fall of 1966, the process seemed to go reasonably well. However, tensions heightened to the point that when the school year began in the late summer of 1970, African-American students protested the lack of diversity on the school's cheerleading squad. During the first football game of the season, a group of six black cheerleaders led cheers for part of the crowd in competition with the school sanctioned squad. The principal, B.E. Miller threatened suspension of the six young women. A group of over 200 marched downtown in protest with some destruction occurring. On Tuesday morning, after the Labor Day holiday, African-American students waited outside the doors of school, waiting to see if the suspensions would be enforced. Miller announced they would and a walkout took place, along with another march.4 The state of emergency by Mayor Whitener followed with a nightly curfew that closed all businesses. Alcohol sales were suspended with Whitener asserting that "a threat to life, health and property now exists within the City of Hickory." A few trashcan fires and two bomb threats shut down the high school on the day of the walkout.5

During the curfew it was mostly white teenagers who were arrested, Police Chief C.L. Hammer observed. He complained that "a lot of young people seemed like they thought the curfew was a joke. They wanted to try us." After six days the ban was lifted. By then, police had found those who set the fires. Additionally, two sixteen-year-olds were arrested for burning a cross in the Ridgeview Cemetery. Slowly, as school reopened, life got back to relative calm around Hickory.6

The city and its people were not blind to the fact that a disparity existed. In their marking of the "All-America City" award, Hickory issued a brochure that dealt fairly honestly with racial issues. Under the title, "Hickory - the problem and the silence," a substantial portion of the text addressed inequality via home ownership and jobs. Much of the acknowledgment was the work of the "bi-racial committee" which showed Hickory had identified the need and intended to address it. The proposed solutions from 1968 included the Hickory Housing Authority, an agency that immediately went to building "220 dwelling units" between the south end of Ridgeview and the Highway 64/70 bypass.7

Many of the amenities Hickory named to secure its "All-America City" title showed the diversity of a city well placed in its region to take on a leadership role for decades to come. Taking the lead in securing those amenities, not only for itself but the area around Hickory became an expectation. "Uniform-united" was how it was described in organizing four counties into a single entity as "a clearinghouse for federal and state grants, and to study and make recommendations concerning area-wide problems, as well as serving as a forum for discussion of those problems." The Western Piedmont Council of Governments (WPCOG) was organized in late 1968 to assist not only Hickory but also all citizens in Catawba, Caldwell, Burke, and Alexander counties with the growing complexity of opportunity in the governmental world of state and nation. That grouping, called collectively the "Unifour," found itself "the fourth largest urban area in North Carolina" and the second fastest growth, at that time. The establishment of WPCOG helped member municipalities and counties collectively plan and protect the region. Since the partnership revolved around Hickory, it only made sense to locate its headquarters there.8

The growth of the area demanded more of everything, including hospitals. Hickory had been served by Richard

Baker Hospital since just after the turn of the century. Down the street, Hickory Memorial opened its doors in 1936, incorporated through the support of George F. Ivey (of Southern Desk) and others. The hospital offered an alternative to Richard Baker, (which became Glenn R. Frye Hospital in 1974). By the 1980s, Hickory Memorial began to specialize in mental health care before eventually becoming a part of Frye Regional Medical Center in 1993.9

But it was a hospital out of town that made news. Since the 1920s, Catawba Memorial Hospital served the population of Newton at its location south of the county seat. In 1962, voters passed a referendum to build a new 4.4 million-dollar facility, with 200 beds. By the time it opened in 1967, it was a six million-dollar hospital. The new Catawba Memorial bought out the old as part of the deal and found itself in Hickory, where the city limits had stretched to encompass it. Near the dividing lines between Hickory, Newton and Conover, the hospital was situated central to Catawba County's three largest municipalities, however at the very eastern end of Hickory. It has changed names along the way becoming Catawba Medical Center in 2002.10

The fast growing nature of Hickory meant new arrivals, some from larger cities expected the same kinds of services they were used to. Frank Drendel, the man who turned CommScope from a small cable manufacturer into a giant in the communications tech world could not believe that Hickory had no cable television. So in 1974, he gathered a group of local investors to build one. The group easily won a franchise from the city to build a system. A year later, subscribers could turn on their TV and get clear channels from Charlotte as well as "superstations" from across the country. They could also receive premium movie channels like HBO. Lines began in Hickory where Catawba Valley Cable TV was headquartered but soon reached across the county, even into Burke.11

Ten years after they first started, the cable company moved to a location on Lenoir-Rhyne Boulevard that provided them the ability to broadcast their own programming. Announced by general manager Wayne Wright in 1984, the company planned to use a segment of CNN Headline News to cablecast a regular news show, six minutes in length at the bottom and top of each hour. In much the same manner, the company interjected local commercials in breaks provided by channels like CNN, TBS, and ESPN.

Once it began, local production blossomed to produce a bunch of programs reflecting the local community. "Catawba Valley Sports Roundup" recapped county high school football and basketball, while "Unifour Racing Update" followed activities at Hickory Motor Speedway. The local crew even broadcast a live race in 1988, with Lenoir-Rhyne College football games and high school basketball tournaments to follow. A show on local history called "Back Then..." aired episodes, some of which were rebroadcast on the History Channel. As a fundraiser for the Hickory Rotary Club, the system aired annual auctions with all the proceeds going to charity.12

Ever since the students of Claremont Central High School left the building to continue their education at the new modern Hickory High School in Viewmont, the city had a problem. What should become of the old building?

The classrooms were then home to a "school for troubled students." The land upon which the old high school stood belonged to Corinth Church. After the demise of Claremont Female College, the church again offered it for educational purposes to Hickory Public Schools. Since 1925, the site hosted the city's high school.13

The arts community seized on the idea of a center that could bring together many of the non-profits in town under one roof. When a group chartered as the Hickory Arts Center, Inc sought use of the building, it became an opportunity for the landmark to live again, this time as a center for culture throughout the region. It made for perfect adaptive reuse and a good marriage to bring many people to the same hill that students came when it was a high school, education.14

The roster of organizations quickly formed. The Hickory Museum of Art was a natural tenant. Continuing to grow in stature and collection, the old gymnasium could offer gallery space in a grand style. The Western Piedmont Symphony, which started as the Hickory Symphony Society, provided another fit. So too did the Hickory Choral Society, a relatively newcomer at the time, which sometimes performed with the backing of portions of the symphony.

The roots of the Symphony go back to the 1940s when Robin Gatwood of Lenoir-Rhyne College put together an ensemble that staged concerts regularly. The group coalesced into the Hickory Symphony Society in 1964, with the former head of the Asheville Symphony coming down the mountain to conduct. By 1972, its musicians and its audience had grown well beyond Hickory, necessitating the name change to Western Piedmont Symphony. By 1972, the organization included the Unifour Youth Symphony to complement the main orchestra, a 55-member body. A number of performance offshoots mark the history of symphonic music in Hickory but by the early 80s a home at the new arts center appealed to the organization.15

The Hickory Choral Society was a much younger group when the center was proposed. They consisted of a wide range of members that went from music majors to others who "just like to sing." Leader Don Coleman brought together 104 voices to offer performances, beginning in 1978. Coleman's mission was to highlight the wealth of vocal talent in the area. When the Hickory Choral Society started he said, "There are a lot of good musicians out there who are just withering on the vine." The all-volunteer ensemble made Monday night rehearsals a ritual as their concerts grew in popularity.16

The roommate for the HCS, HMA, WPS was also relatively new in town. In 1974, a contingent from the Hickory Service League began "looking for donations of anything related to natural history, such as sea shells, butterflies, insects, skeletons, birds' nests and eggs (abandoned only, of course), Indian artifacts, you name it..." The idea was to create a place for children to learn about the natural world. Originally, they called it the "Creative Museum for Youth" but within a few years adopted a new name, the "Catawba Science Museum."17

Together, the arts organizations made for a logical grouping to move to the old facility. Along with the Catawba County Council for the Arts (later known as the

United Arts Council of Catawba County), the new tenants hoped to move into their new home by 1985. Renovation was extensive, beginning two years earlier under the leadership of Harley Shuford, head of the center's board. The 71,764-square foot, neoclassical building began its transformation in 1984, ultimately costing $2.8 million when it opened to the public in the spring of 1986. With a grand celebration, the Arts Center of the Catawba Valley welcomed celebrities like CBS Newsman Charles Kuralt, operatic soprano Roberta Peters, Grammy award winner Roberta Flack, and Howard Edgerton, "inventor of the strobe light." Immediately, the facility went into extensive use with the 500 seat auditorium a regular location for concert performances. In order to remain as inclusive as possible for all its member groups, the Arts Center later changed its name to the SALT Block. The seemingly odd name reflected the coalition that lived in and around the Arts Center. "SALT" stood for "Science, Arts, Literature, Together." Literature indicating the addition of Patrick Beaver Memorial Library, built north of the main building in 1998.18

The one arts organization that was not looking to move into the new arts complex was Hickory Community Theatre. They already had a home that closely fit their needs. Though they considered a move to the Arts Center, HCT director Charles Jeffers noted, "the theater's board of directors had a strong commitment to the (Old City Hall) building and downtown," adding "they felt it would be better to stay here and try to assist this building and try to keep it viable downtown." Once the 1921 City Hall outgrew its facility and decided upon a location on the opposite end (actually a block behind) Union Square, the spacious auditorium became the perfect location for Hickory Community Theater, which has occupied the space ever since.19

Around town, the Arts Center/Salt Block gave Hickoryites many opportunities to be captivated by the arts, science, regularly with exhibits and performances. The center paid off for the community as a beacon, a stalwart example of how rich life could be in Hickory, North Carolina.

Sports too, through Hickory High and Lenoir-Rhyne provided exhilarating moments of competition. But, to some, something was missing. To fully diversify, another option for folks looking for entertainment was needed.

"They look like lobsters. They slink around streams. They don't exactly intimidate the rest of the freshwater crustacean kingdom." That's how two reporters described the name of the new Hickory Class A baseball team's choice when it was announced in late 1992. Though some had suggested taking up the name of the Hickory team from 30 years earlier, times had changed and the use of the term 'Rebel' and all its connection to the divisive issue of slavery from the Civil War prompted owners to start a suggestion campaign for a new designation. General manager of the team Marty Steele, put it simply. "We were looking for a name we could work with." CVCC biology professor Marcia Windham countered any claims the crawdad in nature was less than an interesting creature, saying, "Oh crawdads are all over," adding, "They're not really cute...but they're quick."20

Merchandise, especially hats and shirts could be seen

all around town the summer the Hickory Crawdads took the field for the first time. The newly constructed L.P. Frans Stadium provided a state-of-the-art facility that packed fans to see the "Dads" (a nickname of the nickname) play ball. The effort had been a long standing dream of George Murphy. When he ran for mayor of Hickory in 1977 he made a campaign promise to bring baseball back. He was long out of office when the opportunity came, but nonetheless, he worked hard to make the dream a reality. Murphy's roots in Hickory baseball went all the way back to when he served as play-by-play announcer for the Hickory Rebels. Ten years after his campaign pledge, he embarked on a five-year odyssey of bringing baseball back to town. The effort centered around the stadium itself. According to reporter Greg Trevor, Murphy's pitch to South Atlantic (Sally) League officials received the following response, "build a stadium and you've got your team." Wondering at times if he could pull it off, Murphy and principal investor Don Beaver pitched the idea to a multitude of folks, finally finding a site just off the banks of the Catawba River and gathering the additional financing to build the ballpark.21

Tickets to the games sold faster than any team in the Sally League that first year. At the end of the season, "the Crawdads attracted 283,727 fans," a league record. It was also better than 80 percent of the other minor league teams across the county. A variety of promotions kept casual fans interested. The Crawdads quickly became part of the fabric of the city. In 2018, the team celebrated its 25th anniversary with a sustaining level of support.22

Hickory had become a fully realized city, with hopes

for more. To cap off its achievement as an "All America City," citing its wins and losses, its past glories and future aspirations, folks considered all that had been accomplished. "This is a record of action and of success as Hickory grew in a short time from a small town to a city. Hickory is likely to grow into a major city. This will create more problems and require more answers," conceded the All America City publication. They understood growing pains, they had survived many.23

1   Harold Warren, "Hickory Packs Century Into a Week", Charlotte Observer (CO), June 8, 1970, p. 15.

2   Harold Warren, "Hickory Plans Centennial, CO, March 22, 1970, p. 23A.

3   "Industry of Hickory Hums with Activity", CO, February 21, 1938, p. 14; "Hickory's 'Best Balanced' 'Fastest Growing City in State' Claim Supported by Facts", CO, February 28, 1950, p. 18J; Karen Barber, "Hickory Again Basks In Glory of All America Status", CO, May 19, 1987, Catawba Valley Neighbors Section (Neighbors), p. 1; Richard Maschal, "Hickory Picked as All-America City for 3rd Time", CO, June 9, 2007, p. B2.

4   "Hickory Declares State of Crisis", News & Observer (Raleigh), September 7, 1970, p. 3.

5   "Racial Tension is High" Statesville Record & Landmark, September 9, 1970, p. 1.

6   "School Fired Hit Hickory", CO, September 10, 1970, p. 9; "Hickory Curfew Violator Given Duties at Jail", Charlotte News, September 23, 1970, p. 1.

7   "Hickory, North Carolina: The All America City" (16 page brochure), p. 11-15; "Invitation for Bids", CO, September 12, 1968, p. 6.

8   Charles B. Pegram, "N.C. Unifour Complex Clearing House For Both Federal and State Grants", Rocky Mount Telegram, March 11, 1970, p. 4.

9   "New Corporations" News & Observer (Raleigh), August 26, 1936, p. 5;

"There's a Change in the Air at Hickory Memorial Hospital" CO, September 20, 1987, Neighbors, p. 13; "Frye South Campus: Mental Health and Substance Abuse Programs", CO, December 8, 1996, Special Section, p. 17X; "Name Change Fitting Tribute" (editorial), Statesville Record & Landmark, May 7, 1974, p. 4; "Glenn R. Frye Hospital to Change Name Next Year" CO, September 17, 1983, Neighbors, p. 9.

10   "Bond Vote OKs Hospital For Hickory", CO, July 25, 1962, p. 2; "Catawba Hospital Opens" CO, September 18, 1967, p. 7; "Hospital in tune with the trend", CO, February 10, 2002, Neighbors, p. 20V.

11   Kathi Ann Brown, "Wired to Win: Entrepreneurs of the American Cable Industry", Spectrum Publishing, 2003, p. 76-89.

12   Karen Barber, "Cabling the News", CO, September 6, 1984, Neighbors, p. 9.

13   Karen Barber, "Endowment Expected for Arts Center", CO, April 16, 1986, Neighbors, p. 1; Jane Jeffries, "State Grant to Help Restore School for Arts Center", CO, August 4, 1983, Neighbors, p. 4.

14   Bruce Henderson, "Arts Center Going to Old Hickory High", CO, November 23, 1982, p. B1.

15   https://wpsymphony.org/history/

16   Ken Allen, "Fledgling Hickory Chorus Will Soar on Tuesday", CO, November 17, 1978, p. 9D; https://hickorychoralsociety.org

17   "Tell It Line", CO, October 29, 1974, p. 18B. CO, November 8, 1974, p. 8B; "Catawba Science Center", CO, June 15, 1979, p. 2B.

18   Jody Jaffe, "Catawba Arts Center Ready to Open", CO, April 20, 1986, p. 3F; Karen Barber, "Hickory Takes Wraps Off New Arts Center", CO, April 26, 1986, C1; "Arts council changes its name", CO, June 23, 2006, Neighbors, 2V; "Hickory Celebrates", News & Observer (Raleigh), April 29, 1986, p. 13; "10 Stories to Watch in 1998", CO, December 31, 1997, Neighbors, p. 6V; Shirley Hunter Moore, "Tasty art center name: SALT Block", CO, October 15, 1997, p. 3C.

19   "Theater Drive Moves into Its Final Stage", CO, April 4, 1985, Neighbors, p. 3.

20   Lisa Pollack & John Lennon, "Owners to Christen Baseball Team Today", CO, December 2, 1992, Neighbors, p. 1,3.

21   Greg Trevor, "Anticipation Finally Rewarded", CO, April 17, 1993, p. 7C; "Crawdads Join Lineup in South Atlantic League", CO, April 18, 1993, Special Advertising Section, p. 2X.

22   "Crawdads attendance", CO, October 3, 1993, Neighbors, p. 14V.

23   "Hickory, North Carolina: The All America City" (16 page brochure), p. 16.

T he approach of the sesquicentennial gave Hickory a junction to look back on all that had been accomplished. For a city that spent most of its time moving ahead, the task was for many, rediscovered territory. By some accounts, the last portion of the twentieth century brought tough days to Hickory, but it also brought new beginnings. The trend of offshoring and the loss of jobs it brought, first from the textile and hosiery industry, then furniture, devastated the area. But it was not the first loss.

The entire region recovered from the loss of the furniture market in the 1980s, accepting the loss of an influx of people and commerce that came in the twice yearly market. Not since days of the Great Depression, the crisis of World War II, along with the polio epidemic had Hickory had to tighten its belt and look for other ways to keep people working. One move to heighten hospitality in the city was the ability for restaurants and clubs to offer liquor-by-the-drink as a regular course of service. For years, brown bagging ruled for anyone wishing a cocktail with dinner. The process involved going to a liquor store, buying the alcohol of choice, then taking it to a restaurant, ordering a mixer and pouring the two together. It was supposed to dampen the possibility of inebriation by the public. Often the opposite occurred. The topic remained controversial for years until the North Carolina General Assembly allowed the question to be answered locally. Quick on the heels of Charlotte acceding to mixed drink sales, the whole of Catawba County conducted its own referendum in June of 1979. The measure failed county wide. Hickory mayor Bill McDonald lamented the defeat, saying "we're going to see a demise in our economy." He pointed to fears that the prohibition would cause the Western North Carolina furniture industry to "move its markets from Hickory and Catawba County to High Point, which has liquor by the drink."[1]

He was prescient but not for the reason he cited. Plus, Hickory was not done with the issue. City leaders in Hickory and nearby Conover noticed that the yes votes were in the majority in their municipalities. A year later, mixed drink proponents tried again, limiting the question to the two cities. This time the referendum passed by a 2 to 1 margin in Hickory and over 60 percent in Conover. Liquor-by-the-drink was not enough to keep the furniture market in Hickory, but it did open up the city to numerous new restaurants, established in the wake of the change.[2]

A variety of nightclubs had come and gone in Hickory, even before mixed drink sales. Popular places like Fast Company on the west side, Eli's 2 on the south side or in Viewmont, Someplace Else and Yesterday's featured a growing band scene, showcasing local and regional musicians every weekend. Those clubs could offer beer and wine but no mixed drinks. In the late 1980s Club Cabaret opened in downtown Hickory. The gay bar quickly became a popular venue for competitions by male and female impersonators from around not only the Catawba Valley region, but the entire southeastern United States.[3]

One important outgrowth of the mixed-drink vote was the creation of the Hickory Metro Convention Center. A partnership of the two cities where the referendum passed, the Hickory-Conover Tourism Development Authority selected a patch of land just off Interstate 40 in 1986. It took ten years to build, given costs and some controversy about the site of the center so far away from downtown Hickory. However, by the time the convention center opened in 1997, concerns had evaporated when the Hickory Downtown Development Association supported the move. The facility began to elevate the economy of the area with regular attractions. The first event booked was appropriately enough, a furniture suppliers trade show, in the days just before several high profile furniture companies moved their manufacturing operations out of the country. 4

Construction of the convention center for $6.5 million came with a public-private partnership headed by Leroy Lail. His suggestion of a five percent occupancy tax to fund operations of the largest convention space between Charlotte and Asheville helped keep the facility underwritten, along with fees from the various conventions who come to town, creating a "win-win" for the Hickory economy. Hickory city taxpayers did not have to fund the Metro Center, those visiting did, as well as spending their money in the local economy, a much needed boost as the twenty-first century dawned.5

By the 1980s Hickory looked like a more metropolitan place, able to attract a variety of constituencies within the region. The borders of the Unifour, Catawba, Burke, Caldwell and Alexander counties had grown into the fourth largest metropolitan area, behind Charlotte, Raleigh and the Triad of Winston-Salem, Greensboro, High Point. The term "Unifour" no longer properly denoted what was going on within it. The Western Piedmont Council of Governments recognized the dilemma, and began promoting the area as the "Hickory Metro," a quick, easy way to define the region. The economic development community began to use the term extensively. Hickory had found itself in the middle of a region recognized as important to the state of North Carolina.6

Even with the loss of the furniture market, Hickory offered a lot of activity. Both downtown and along the bypass, a unique coterie of businesses sprang up. One example was Union Plaza News. Robert Canipe started the magazine and newspaper store in downtown Hickory in 1986, offering books, magazines, comics, and collectibles, especially baseball cards for a varied clientele. He likened his business to "the old general store, except we don't have a pot-bellied stove." Customers came in and talked with Canipe for hours about a variety of subjects, everything from Superman to Corvettes to the Peloponnesian War. Two years later he opened "Hickory's finest comic shop," in Valley Hills Mall, renaming all locations "Amazing Heroes".7

Canipe's expanding comic book and magazine empire reflected the growth of the city.

Many businesses were scaling up, both large and small. One Hickory company pushed its operations to the very limits of the city, into a new county.

Alex and Lee George had been in the grocery business all their lives, as part of their father Moses' stores in Shelby and Lincolnton. When Alex graduated from Duke, he and his little brother set out to follow family tradition. In 1931, they bought "Merchants Produce, a wholesale food business in Hickory." The brothers, with the eventual help of their father and their sister, Josephine, grew the business to the point that in the late 1950s a huge warehouse was needed. Along the 321 corridor, just across the road from the Hickory Home Furnishings Mart, MDI built a new facility. They added space to it regularly, including a site for Institutional Food House, their distribution outlet for restaurants. But by the 1980s, the company grew beyond its capacity again. In the mid-90s, MDI found a tract of land big enough to locate its plan for a 956,000 square-foot warehouse, just across the river, in Caldwell County. Undeterred, the city expanded its boundaries into the next county to provide needed services to the company that began in a small building in downtown Hickory.8

One of Hickory's landmark amenities had been its community center. Build in the late early post-World War II era, the recreational complex provided children and adults alike with fun and exercise. The Hickory Foundation Community Center, located just north of the Frye Regional Medical Center complex even served as the gymnasium for Hickory High and Lenoir-Rhyne. It was there that Hickory basketball fans watched L-R defeat UNC-Chapel Hill in basketball in 1949. The score was 79-78. As a further link to L-R, Joe Bear, a live cub was housed at the Community Center as part of a larger zoo, that kept a monkey (that smoked) and a lion, as well as other animals. Always central to the livelihood of Hickory, in 1994 the Community Center was renovated and became part of the county's YMCA facilities. Capital campaigns added such pluses as an aquatic center, wellness center and child development center. In addition, the C.O. Miller Teen Center opened in 2005, named for the longtime director that many Hickory teens say helped to raise them. The Hickory Foundation YMCA serves a diverse group every day with facilities for a wide range of activities to strengthen body, mind, and spirit.

As Hickory expanded, fears that much of the "old" Hickory was disappearing became a topic of conversation. The effort to preserve one historic landmark sparked the creation of an enduring preservation organization, the Hickory Landmarks Society (HLM). When the Propst House, a Victorian home had become vacant, was deteriorating and threatened with demolition, a group of concerned citizens banded together to save the structure. They formed the nucleus of the organization that was to follow. By 1970, the house was moved to a safe location and before the end of the decade, it had been restored for visitation, allowing twentieth century Hickory to see how nineteenth century Hickory lived. Following the success of the Propst House, HLM bought Maple Grove, Dolph Shuford's home, restoring it for tours and as the organization's headquarters. Since then HLM has participated in numerous projects, helping homeowners preserve historic homes in Hickory for use as living space. Besides Propst and Maple Grove, HLM saved Houk's Chapel, a Methodist church built in 1893 that was thought to have been used by Lutheran and Baptist congregations as well. In addition, the organization works with private parties to preserve structures around the city, adapting them for use into the future.9

The other historic home in Hickory fell to the Historical Association of Catawba County to preserve. The Newton-based group took over the home Daniel Shuler built in 1887, and later owned by Elizabeth C. Thornton and her husband Col. Marcellus E., and the Finley Gwyn Harper family. In 2000, the HACC took over the property and commenced a campaign to endow the estate. By the end of 2001, tours began with a plea to the public to help identify the silhouettes found on the third floor, the requirements of entry during the days of Prohibition. Among principal donors to the restoration of the house for touring was the Hickory Merchants Association, contributing $300,000 to the $2 million effort.10

Preservation of a different kind started at the Hickory Municipal Airport in 2007. A group called the Sabre Society began the Hickory Aviation Museum, but their roots went back to 1991 when they took possession of a Navy FJ3 Fury and began restoring it. One plane led to another until the museum proudly displayed "an F-4 Phantom, an A-7 Corsair, and an F-14 Tomcat of 'Top Gun' fame,' among others. 11

With big city attractions came big city problems. By 1983, the Family Guidance Center celebrated its 25th year of helping family and individuals cope with strains and mental health issues. In the 1970s, the public assistance organization moved into the old Catawba County Health Department building on the 64/70 bypass, and expanded from family counseling to a fully diversified agency, offering programs regularly on everything from credit counseling to parenting and grief. Big Brothers/Big Sisters, a volunteer group to mentor school age children was one of the many ongoing services offered as the Family Guidance Center broadened its horizons to meet the need.12

The end of the twentieth century brought a number of challenges to Hickory. Several sensational legal events kept readers involved in the twists and turns of justice in Hickory. In 1987, an African-American man was arrested and later convicted of a rape for which he was later exonerated. Ten years later, a trial involving charges of murder and conspiracy enthralled the public for months in what turned out to be the longest trial in Catawba County history. The public followed with rapt attention the unfolding tale of an exotic dancer charged with conspiracy to commit the murder of her estranged husband with another man who, when cornered took his own life. Ultimately, she was acquitted but denied custody of her child in a saga that played during 1997.13

Like the floods of 1916 and 1940, another natural disaster caused extensive damage when Hurricane Hugo passed over western North Carolina just as the summer of 1989 was turning to autumn. Most of the damage came with winds that gusted up to 85 miles per hour. Trees toppled causing widespread power outages that lasted weeks for some folks. Torrents of rain hit the area too but the intensity of the storm weakened as it passed through.14

A storm of a different kind enveloped the entire nation, but did particular damage to Hickory's reputation. A 2016 report by Castlight Health cited Hickory as the fifth worst city in the nation of opioid abuse. The allegation portrayed citizens unable to deal with job loss in the area turning to prescription abuse to handle the bleak employment landscape. But the designation did not ring true with the Hickory Police Department, who were not seeing the number of calls that a city so blighted by such an epidemic would experience. Immediately, Deputy Chief Reed Baer dug into the numbers and found a bias that skewed the numbers.

Major Baer found that the study did not take into account the presence of two major pharmacies in town that dispensed opioids for nursing homes across the state. The pills were not staying in Hickory. Also, the report only included 13 states, so it was not a nationwide look at the problem. Baer found Hickory was the ninth largest metropolitan statistical area in the state. Yet the city ranked sixteenth in NC for for cases of opioid related incidents, according to the state's department of health and human services, thus revealing the city had fewer cases than expected for its size. Unfortunately, when the news hit, giving Hickory the dubious distinction of fifth in the nation, the followup analysis never made the same kind of splash, instead tagging Hickory as something that it was not.5

§

Some of the anxiety that led to opioid addiction came from the job market in Hickory. It was shrinking. Downturns in the economy caused employers to trim their payrolls before, but what happened as the twenty-first century took hold in the area, spelled real trouble for the Hickory economy. Experiencing "the nation's third highest increase in unemployment," the culprit was the move of two pillars of Hickory's industrial base moving their operations off shore, textiles and furniture. By 2001, textile firms as major area employers was largely gone. The real shock came when furniture went away as well. Over the coming decade, jobs continued to bleed away, with 2007 being a particularly tough year. While the rest of the state rebounded somewhat, the hemorrhage continued as Hickory was identified as the only metro area to lose jobs.16

Retraining became the answer to a reduction in Hickory's industrial workforce. Classes at Catawba Valley Community College filled beyond capacity during that time with many displaced workers looking for their next career. During that time a new president took the seat at CVCC. Dr. Garrett D. Hinshaw came with a new focus for the college. Riding the wave of new and returning students, he looked for new ways to train professionals for a variety of jobs. Thinking furniture was a part of Catawba County's past he closed the furniture program. But within a few years, he noticed a change. Manufacturers were bringing back some of those jobs and in partnership with those companies, CVCC established the Furniture Academy, a focused training program for a resurgent furniture industry.

But Hinshaw's first big move was to recognize a need in the health care industry that his community college could fill. He began to convert the fifth floor of the Hickory campus' newly constructed building into a simulated hospital training facility. "The creation of the ValleySim Hospital at CVCC was the first step in signifying that the college recognized the value of quality healthcare in Hickory," assessed Hinshaw after completion. He added, "this innovative idea to create a hospital environment that could be used exclusively for training demonstrated that the college was going to turn itself inside out for the betterment of the community." With the oncoming of the opioid epidemic and the aging of the baby boomers, the training facility bolstered health care in and around Hickory. Called the most state-of-the-art medical training facility built by a community college this side of the Mississippi, CVCC's Sim Hospital trained students in everything from gunshot wounds to births thanks to "high-tech mannequins" that react like humans.17

CVCC had always been nimble when it came to the needs of the area's workforce. Dr. Hinshaw's next big idea was to "send a message to the community, existing businesses, and to prospective new business recruits that the Catawba Valley Region is serious about providing a talented workforce for its stakeholders." In 2018, he oversaw construction of the CVCC Workforce Solutions Center. The complex houses training for a variety of industries including mechatronics, machining, automotive, welding, and 3D printing, among others. As Hinshaw has noted, "It not only inspires economic development, it also serves as a signal to young people that there are great technology driven opportunities here in Catawba County for their future careers."18

Another educational outlet was also changing in Hickory. As Lenoir-Rhyne added programs and campuses, by 2008, it had outgrown the designation of "college." A move by the college's board of trustees voted to change its appellation to "Lenoir-Rhyne University," stating that the new name "better reflects the expanded offerings the college is planning to pursue." The school immediately went about improving its student center and student housing, as well

as constructing a new science complex with a price tag of
$50 million. Four years later, L-R merged with a Columbia,
South Carolina seminary and offered graduate classes in
Asheville.19

A whole host of landmarks were changing in Hickory.
Along Lenoir-Rhyne Boulevard, the five-lane thoroughfare
that brought students and their parents to the university
from Interstate 40, several unused and decaying hosiery
mills still showing the blight caused by the loss of the
industry. In 2013, both Moretz Mills and Hollar Mill, one
block from each other, gained new life. The two structures,
both on the National Register of Historic Places, were gutted
with the idea to bring them back to the public's attention
with a variety of retail attractions including restaurants.
The following year another organization invested over $7
million to do bring back another historic mill in Hickory.
The old Lyerly Mill, which dated back to the 1930s was
rehabilitated as the new campus for Transportation Insight,
a logistics company. In the same area, five years before, the
Granary, also located near Lenoir-Rhyne was repurposed for
office space. The conversions spelled new opportunities for
buildings that outlived their initial use.20

Perhaps the site in Hickory to which citizens of the
world knew the city for was not a historic building but a
new one, overlooking Interstate 40. The four story complex
housed the world headquarters for Comm/Scope, a cable
manufacturer that exemplified the appeal of living and doing
business in Hickory.

The genesis of the company goes back to 1953, when
"the Hickory Development Corporation, an offshoot of the

Chamber of Commerce" attracted a group of entrepreneurs from Superior Cable Corporation in downtown Hickory. The company offered a new product to the local workforce, telephone wire. Selling its product to the Hickory Telephone and a host of other phone companies, it was ultimately acquired by Continental Telephone, which developed another product for use, coaxial cable, or "coax" in a division they called CommScope. Primarily used by the cable television industry, the idea of television via cable wire had not yet caught on across the country. CommScope had a product nobody wanted. Management at Continental sought to sell the coax manufacturer, which had a plant in Sherrill's Ford. They sent ambitious and young Frank Drendel to Hickory to find a buyer.21

Born in Illinois, Drendel worked his way through college installing telephones. He convinced his wife, Pinky to move from sunny Southern California to Hickory as he took on the job of selling the coax maker. It was not an easy task. Mrs. Drendel did not relish the idea of moving to a place she had never heard of, but a small earthquake helped change her mind about California, and she agreed to travel with Frank.

With the housing market of Hickory tight in 1974, the Drendels moved into a double-wide trailer for a period of time, while Frank Drendel evaluated the operation. He saw something he liked. Fully confident the cable television industry would grow, he wanted to purchase the company himself. Drendel made friends easily and it wasn't long until he amassed a group of local investors to finance the purchase of Comm/Scope. He also talked them into creating a cable television system in Hickory, finding none there when he got to town.

Drendel bet on consumers appreciating the options of cable above antenna reception for viewing. HBO was just the first of many cable channels for which television viewers began to clamor in the 1970s. Within a year, he had turned CommScope from a company losing money to a profit maker. With his vision, energy and ability to find good partners, Frank Drendel established CommScope as a leader in coaxial, as well as fiber optic cable.22

One of CommScope's investors, the French manufacturer that came to be known as Alcatel also located in Hickory, as did Siecor, a merger of Siemens and Corning. All three competed for contracts to supply the lines cable companies strung from pole to home. The wiring of the American household had strong ties to Hickory. While Alcatel and Corning (Siecor's successor) have left Hickory, (Corning still manufactures in Hickory, but the corporate offices have moved to Charlotte) the $9 billion Comm/Scope still centers its operations in Hickory, and Frank Drendel considers the growth of the company among his crowning achievements. That's quite a statement for the man who made C-Span possible and won an Emmy Award for providing HBO with its encryption system.23

Frank Drendel came to a town blessed with leadership that believed Hickory's best days were still to come. Julian Whitener was coming to the end of his tenure as mayor that dated back to the 1950s. So beloved and respected was Whitener, that the new city hall was named for him. George Murphy followed Whitener into the mayor's chair for a four year stint.

Bill McDonald was mayor for twenty years, from 1981-2001. During his five terms, the tax base grew from 160 million to four billion dollars. Mayor McDonald always looked forward to challenges calling them "opportunities in work clothes."

Following McDonald's retirement, Rudy Wright won election next, serving for 16 years. Characterized as an "enthusiastic ambassador" for his city, he was the chief driver of the passage of the bond that has allowed the city to invest in itself with the Hickory Trail. Wright died in 2017 during his fourth term in office, but his legacy remains. His widow, Donna Wright thought it was the perfect job for him, one that he threw himself into 150%. She referred to her late husband as someone who loved people and believed Hickory's best days were ahead of them, just like previous generations.4

When Rudy Wright died unexpectedly, the city turned to another stalwart to lead the city. Former city council member and well known businessman Jeff Cline accepted the job to fill out Wright's term, admirably helping to see Wright's vision through to the next election. Two years later, the city elected Hank Guess to the job. Mayor Guess had been a lifelong servant to the people of Hickory as an officer, later lieutenant in the Hickory Police Department and member of the city council. He also shared the former mayors' belief in the need to aggressively craft a new city from the old.25

With each generation, leadership has stepped up to serve, ready for innovation to propel Hickory forward. The contributions of a wide range of people, from business, education, social and governmental sectors, which sometimes overlapped, provide a framework from which the next achievement could be launched, putting the city in good stead for tomorrow.

1   "Mixed Drink Proposal Loses in Catawba", CO, June 6, 1979, p. 2B.

2   "Mixed Drinks Approved", CO, September 10, 1980, p. 2B.

3   Jen Aronoff, "Crowning the Drag Kings", CO, October 7, 2005, p. 3E.

4   Andrew Shain, "'It's a relief': New civic center to open", CO, March 9, 1997, p. 1V, 16V.

5   Tony Mecia, "Cities Find Their Centers" CO, March 12, 2000, p. 1L, 6L; Leroy Lail, "Win-Win", Redhawk Publications, 2020, chapter 8.

6   Tom Bradbury, "The 4th metro", CO, June 26, 1993, p. 16A.

7   "In Business: Robert Canipe", CO, January 2, 1987, Neighbors, p. 9; "Writers to hold book signing", CO, September 19, 2001, p. 2V; "Mall Has A New Look With 16 New Retailers", CO, December 24, 1989, Neighbors, p. 26.

8   Val Maiewskij-Hay & Chris Roush, "Delivering on Values: The Story of Alex Lee", 2006, Fenwick Publishing, p. 33, 169; https://gis.catawbacountync.gov/maps/HickoryCity.pdf

9   Gayle Tuttle, "Hickory Ready to Open Propst House, CO, May 15, 1979, p. B1; http://www.hickorylandmarks.org/PropstHouse.asp; http://www.hickory-landmarks.org/History.asp; http://www.hickorylandmarks.org/HouksChapel.asp

10   Hannah Mitchell, "Grand old home in Hickory will be new history museum", CO, October 29, 2000, p. V1; "Merchants group gives to campaign" CO, September 16, 2001, p. 6V; Hannah Mitchell, "Attic art portrays mystery guests", CO, November 18, 2001, p. 13B.

11   Mary Elizabeth DeAngelis, "Navy Fury jet makes one last flight", CO, October 30, 1991, p. C1; Joe Marusak, "War memories take flight", CO, May 2, 2007, p. V1; Chanda Blitch, "Combat aircraft land at Hickory airport", CO, August 22, 2007, p. V1, V2.

12   "Credit Counseling", CO, August 14, 1983, Neighbors, p. 7; Karen Barber, "Soon-To-Be Parents Get Education in Living With Babies", CO, September 4, 1983, Neighbors, p. 4; Karen Barber, "Family Guidance Center Plans Long Lived 25th Birthday Party", CO, May 26, 1983, Neighbors, p. 6; CO, November 29, 1998, p. 12V.

13   "The Unifour's top ten stories of 1997" CO, December 31, 1997, p. 6V; "$3.25M awarded innocent man's 24 years in prison", News & Observer (Raleigh), August 26, 2018, p. A3.

14   Jordan Hensley, "Looking back on Hurricane Hugo in Hickory, 29 years later", HDR, September 11, 2018, https://www.hickoryrecord.com/news/looking-back-on-hurricane-hugo-in-hickory-years-later/article_b81081fc-b53c-11e8-b301-b726030b94c1.html.

15   https://www.hickoryrecord.com/news/opinion-hickory-s-opioid-problem-our-crisis/article_1862cb56-8b08-11e7-93b1-37c3da23eeb3.html; https://www.hickoryrecord.com/news/fight-against-the-opioid-crisis-on-home-front-in-hickory/article_d1b8e879-e7e1-524a-b2bb-464a8e4ebcf2.html; Kevin Griffin, "Catawba County received 67.3 million opioid pills in 7 years. That's the equivalent of 62 pills per person per year", HDR, July 24, 2019, https://www.hickoryrecord.com/news/catawba-county-received-67-3-million-opioid-pills-in-7-years-thats-the-equivalent-of/article_aadfb282-ae47-11e9-8f54-332fb71fa851.html; https://www.northcarolinahealthnews.org/2017/07/27/four-north-carolina-cities-make-top-25-list-opioid-abuse/; https://naminc.org/nc-communities-work-together-combat-opioid-epidemic/; Telephone interview with Chief Thurman Whisnant and Major Reed Baer, June 10, 2020.

16   Adam Bell, "Catawba Valley residents feel the pain of job loss", CO, May 13, 2001, p. 6B.

17   CO, October 2, 2011, p. V3; Dianne Straley, "Simulated hospital improves nurses training", CO, November 27, 2011, p. L1; Interview with Dr. Garrett D. Hinshaw, May 2020.

18   Interview with Dr. Garrett D. Hinshaw, May 2020; http://www.cvcc.edu/Academic-Resources/Programs/Industrial/Workforce-Solutions-Complex.cfm

19   Michelle Crouch, "Lenoir-Rhyne trades its 'College' for 'University', CO, March 17, 2008, p. 14; Marcie Young, "Name change for Lenoir-Rhyne, College will become 'University' this fall", CO, March 20, 2008, V1, V7; April Bethea, "Lenoir-Rhyne to Merge with Lutheran seminary", CO, March 28, 2012, B1; CO,

August 5, 2012, p. V1.

20   Charlene H. Carpenter, "Moretz Mills gets new life", CO, October 13, 2013, p. 1V, 4V.

21   Kathi Ann Brown, "Connecting: The CommScope Story", Spectrum Publishing, 2006, p. 5-7.

22   Kathi Ann Brown, "Wired to Win: Entrepreneurs of the American Cable Industry", Spectrum Publishing, 2003, p, 76-89.

23

24   https://www.hickoryrecord.com/news/former-hickory-mayor-dies/article_e408a5ee-d86b-11e3-a3d0-0017a43b2370.html; https://www.wfae.org/post/family-late-hickory-mayor-rudy-wright-sees-lessons-his-suicide#stream/0; https://www.hickorync.gov/content/city-council; Telephone interview with Donna Wright, June 15, 2020, Hickory, NC.

25   https://www.ncleg.net/Sessions/2007/Bills/Senate/HTML/S1568v0.html; https://www.hickoryrecord.com/opinion/bluntness-was-part-of-former-mayors-persona/article_2c885664-37ce-5a89-868a-3c3a7b47c0f6.html; https://www.hickorync.gov/content/bill-mcdonald-scholarship-fund

About Richard Eller

"I believe the past is an essential portal for understanding of the present, which helps us determine our future," commented Richard Eller about the value of history. Since he was young, the images of the past have always held a fascination for Eller, who in 2015 became the Catawba Valley Community College Historian in Residence for the Historical Association of Catawba County. He has delved into important historical events to make them relevant and understandable to a current audience.

In the early 1990s as Production Manager with Hickory, NC's cable television franchise, he began a documentary series called *Back Then...* which presented stories of the area. In all, seventeen episodes of the series were produced with two segments aired on the History Channel. The series won the Partnership Award for its work with historical organizations by the North Carolina Cable Television Association.

Eller's formal writing career began with an examination of the fabled origins of Abraham Lincoln. With co-author Jerry Goodnight, he delved into a long held belief that the 16th president of the United States was actually a North Carolinian by birth, a secret Lincoln himself sought to conceal as a way to avoid being labeled 'illegitimate.' The sensation caused by *The Tarheel Lincoln* gained the notice of CNN, the Chicago Tribune and other media outlets across the nation in 2004.

As a kid growing up in Winston-Salem, NC Eller was familiar with Piedmont Airlines so it was a thrill to take on the task of telling the story of the remarkable airline. In 2008, he authored *Piedmont Airlines: A Complete History*, following it up with a feature length documentary, *Speedbird: The History of Piedmont*

Airlines. The documentary was featured on PBS North Carolina and the book won an award by the North Carolina Society of Historians.

To examine the polio epidemic of 1944, which Eller believes constituted the most consequential historical event to occur in Catawba County, he gathered a group of colleagues together to produce a book and companion documentary on the subject. Interviewing survivors of the devastating, yet inspiring event along with rarely seen footage and day-by-day activity at the hospital, he and his coauthors reveal a story that continues to demonstrate resilience in the face of an unseen viral killer.

The tale of the *Untouchables,* a 1964 high school football team that shutout every opponent became the topic of his next quest. The team from Hickory's only African-American high school was known in its community but much less so outside. Eller worked to change that. Through a feature length documentary the story became known to the United Arts Council of Catawba County, who then secured a public arts grant to commemorate the team and the high school at the site where the team played. Scheduled for release in 2021, the story has already been the subject of segments on WBTV (with its renewed Carolina Camera show) and PBS North Carolina.

Eller continues to search out and present important stories about the lives of those who made the Catawba Valley what it is today. Recently, he completed a thorough history of the city of Hickory, and is currently writing a history of the western North Carolina furniture industry, tentatively titled *Industry in the Wood.* Always interested in the trials and triumphs of those who went before us, he is a frequent contributor to Foothills Digest, a magazine about the area, as well as biographies about Hickory entrepreneur Leroy Lail and the Hickory Furniture Mart.

At CVCC, he directs the activities of a new venture that harmonizes with his research activity. In 2017, he and Editor-in-Chief Robert Canipe began Redhawk Publications (now Redhawk Creative Solutions), a campus press with a twofold purpose. The enterprise seeks to help faculty create scaffolding workbooks and texts designed to help students comprehend course objectives and the material in their respective classes. To date, over a dozen works by instructors have resulted in better performance by students in their coursework. Additionally, Redhawk has published works by its community stakeholders to present and inform readers about the area. In conjunction with CVCC's graphic arts programs, Redhawk has published works on the Henry River Mill Village, the cities of both Newton and Hickory (*Newton:Then & Now* and *Hickory:Then & Now*), as well as numerous works of fact and fiction by writers in the Catawba Valley, including Eller himself. Redhawk is also starting a video program to assist those interested in telling their own story with film. Inaugural classes begin in 2021.

Eller remains in the classroom teaching history to help the next generation gain an appreciation of past as they prepare for the future. Getting outside the four walls of a classroom has been a priority. In 2004, he started *HandsOnHistory*, an initiative that takes students to sites where history happened. Gettysburg, Valley Forge, Selma, Memphis, all across Europe and North Carolina too have been destinations for classes. "It is important for students to see an enthusiastic and informed presentation of the past," said Eller adding, "it helps them to connect, internalize and map a future that will make their world better."

With a Masters of History from the University of North

Carolina at Charlotte, Eller's undergraduate degree is from Lenoir-Rhyne University. He is married to Claudia Ward-Eller, the father of two children, who themselves have two, making him the grandfather of four beautiful kids whom he hopes will be carriers of history into the next generation. An avid traveler, he follows his passion for history to some of America's best known and well-hidden historic sites, looking for his next research subject. "Harry Truman was right," Eller said. "The only new thing in the world is the history we don't know yet."

www.ingramcontent.com/pod-product-compliance
Lightning Source LLC
Chambersburg PA
CBHW072145270326
41931CB00010B/1895